Journey By Stages

JOURNEY BY STAGES

*Some Account of the People
who Travelled by
Stage-Coach and Mail
in the Years between
1660 and 1840*

by

STELLA MARGETSON

CASSELL · LONDON

CASSELL & COMPANY LTD
35 Red Lion Square, London WC1
Melbourne, Sydney, Toronto
Johannesburg, Cape Town, Auckland

© *Stella Margetson 1967*
First published 1967

PRINTED IN GREAT BRITAIN
BY EBENEZER BAYLIS AND SON LIMITED
THE TRINITY PRESS, WORCESTER, AND LONDON
F. 267

With Love to Dear Georgina

ACKNOWLEDGEMENTS

I would like to acknowledge my great debt to the authors and publishers of the more recent books listed in the Bibliography at the end of this volume.

I wish to thank in particular all the editors of the Diaries, Journals and Letters which have been the main source of my material; Mr Edmund Vale for unearthing the Mail Coach Superintendent's correspondence in *The Mail Coach Men of the Late Eighteenth Century* (Cassell & Co. Ltd.); Mr Leslie Gardiner for information about coach travelling in Scotland in *Stage Coach to John o'Groats* (Hollis & Carter Ltd.); Mr Malcolm Letts for introducing me to some of the foreign visitors to Britain in *As the Foreigner Saw Us* (Methuen & Co. Ltd.); and Mr N. C. Selway for his book on the coaching prints of James Pollard, *The Regency Road* (Faber & Faber Ltd.).

I would also like to thank the staff of the Guildhall Library and the British Museum for their help in tracing the documents and books of an earlier date relevant to my subject; Miss Vera Douie, the indefatigable Librarian of the Fawcett Library, for all her kindness, and my friend, Mrs G. M. Ahearn, for allowing me to spend many happy hours hunting my travellers through the books in her library. Nor shall I ever cease to be grateful for the encouragement given to me in the early stages of writing this book by the late Peter Watt.

CONTENTS

LIST OF ILLUSTRATIONS

1

EARLY
TRAVELLERS

WHEN THE FIRST stage-coaches appeared on the road
in the middle of the seventeenth century, England was
still a rural country. Rolling hills and pasturelands,
open fields, forests and thickets stretched for miles
between her sea coasts, with here and there an isolated
farm or a small village clustered round its church and
manor house. The small market towns, the seaports and
the cathedral cities had a life of their own, often quite
cut off from their neighbours when the dark blind of
winter descended on them and even in the summer
linked only by the most primitive forms of transport.
London had a population of some 250,000, considered in
those days to be an enormously high figure. The country
came right up to its gates; cows were pastured in Islington and sweet fields of corn grew on the way to
Hampstead. The River Thames was still the great
highway from the City to Westminster and public
transport dominated by its rumbustious watermen.

But coaches—so called because they were first made
at Kotze, a small town in Hungary—had been introduced into Britain one hundred years earlier by a
Dutchman. They were uncomfortable, cumbersome

contraptions with heavy bodies on very small wheels and no springs. Queen Elizabeth I, though of all women the most forward-looking and courageous, disliked them intensely. After riding in one designed for her by Walter Rippon, she quite firmly and flatly refused ever to sit in it again; and it was not until after the Armada that she consented to be driven to St Paul's for the service of thanksgiving in a very elaborate new state coach made in the shape of a gaudy pumpkin on wheels. Pride in the glorious triumph of her sea-captains may have helped her to ignore the fact that the coach swayed and rattled up Ludgate Hill worse than any ship on the ocean: with 'the heart and the stomach of a king', she could endure most things.

Not so, the counsellors and courtiers who surrounded her. They suffered from her royal commands and endured great pains in journeying about the kingdom on her behalf, knowing full well that in her hey-day she could outride the best of them, galloping ahead with her favourite, the Earl of Leicester, or riding pillion behind her Chamberlain on a magnificently caparisoned stallion. Only when age and feebleness crept up on royal majesty was the great Queen persuaded to give up riding, and even then she preferred being carried in a well-cushioned litter or sailing in the royal barge to being driven in the hated coach.

Travel by land from one point to another still retained the meaning of its biblical origin—travail. It was dangerous, difficult and exhausting. Noblemen with large country estates and rich merchants living in the cities travelled from necessity, not for pleasure, and never in the winter if their journey could be avoided. They dared not set out without a retinue of attendants to help them find their way and to protect them from the bands of robbers waiting in ambush on the lonely roads. Anyone was fair game, whether travelling on horseback or—a rare sight—by one of the new-fangled coaches imported from abroad. These indeed excited the utmost curiosity and a fearful trepidation. When the cultured and sophisticated Earl of Arundel brought a coach over from Germany for his own private use, the simple townspeople and villagers of Sussex believed that the great ornate vehicle, painted crimson and black with a blazing torch motif embossed on the roof, could only have come from the regions of Hell and that his lordship was bewitched.

Six strong horses with a postilion riding one of the leaders and a coachman driving the other four, were required to drag the heavy coach through the foul ways from the Earl's castle at Arundel to his town house in the Strand and the journey took several days. Travellers in a hurry much preferred riding on horseback and they favoured the post-horse system of journeying, whereby fresh horses could be hired for stages marked out by inns along the road and changed at them. Messengers carrying important letters of state went immense distances in the shortest possible time in this way. Sir Robert Cary after the death of Queen Elizabeth, eager to acclaim King James IV of Scotland as King James I of England, set up a record by riding from London to Edinburgh, a distance of 400 miles, in three days. Leaving the Queen's bedside at nine in the morning, he covered 162 miles to Doncaster before nightfall, riding a further 136 miles to his own home in Northumberland on the second day and reaching Edinburgh the following night after a serious fall, which made it necessary for him to ride the last lap 'softly'. When he arrived he was caked in mud and dust and quite unrecognizable, but King James rewarded him with a peerage.

Ordinary people from the towns and villages of England hardly did any travelling at all. Their lives were centred upon the aristocratic families who owned the land, or were concerned with the local guilds in the towns and cities, where the craftsmen and traders pooled their resources and organized themselves into a strong self-supporting community. If they did have to travel and they could not afford to hire a horse, they walked, or they used the huge waggons and market carts that made their way across country at a snail's pace. Few of them ever ventured any distance, except as servants attending on their masters.

But by the beginning of the seventeenth century some progress towards fulfilling the needs of ordinary people had been made. In London a few enterprising traders began to hire out coaches at a fee of 10s. a day for short distances on the 'stones', as the cobbled streets of the city were known. Called hackney coaches, because they were drawn by two slow-moving, common horses best described by the French word *hacquenée*, they looked like an enlarged treasure chest on wheels. The windows had no glass in them but were protected by a shutter, which could be lowered in fine weather with a mat conveniently thrown over it for passengers leaning out of the carriage to rest their elbows in comfort.

In the country a new 'long-waggon' was introduced for transporting people as well as goods. Twenty passengers could be carried by it at the rate of 15 miles a day in stages, standing up or sitting on the floor on a thin layer of straw, which failed entirely to cushion them against the appalling state of the roads; for England, leading the world in the traffic on the high seas, had fallen far behind her European neighbours in road-making. The lessons taught by the Romans had long been forgotten and the great highways linking one city with another utterly neglected, where they had not been plundered by the local gentry for stone and rubble to build new houses for themselves and their tenants. Road repairing was done by children of four and five years old,

hired by the farmers to collect stones from the surrounding fields and drop them into the ruts ploughed up by
the wheels of the heavy carts and waggons, and this
treatment only made the way more hazardous for the
traveller on horseback, since the loose stones flying out
of the pot-holes could blind or otherwise injure both
horse and rider. After rain the so-called roads were a
sticky sea of mud; in dry weather they disappeared in a
tornado of dust that settled in a thick ridge along the
wayside. A rider with a lame horse, alone in the country,
was a lost man.

Nothing much was done to improve matters during the
reign of King Charles I, and the tragic conflict between
the King and Parliament put additional fear into the
heart of the peaceful traveller, who might find himself
caught up on the wrong side of the opposing armies,
cut off from his home by Prince Rupert's cavalry or
pinned inside the walls of a city by Cromwell's Ironsides.
Sir William Waller, for instance, could not reach Osterley
Park, near Hounslow, while Prince Rupert was sweeping
on from Brentford to Turnham Green, and Lady Verney
had the greatest difficulty in getting home to Claydon
from London: mounted on 'a sorry nagg' which was all
she could get, she found Uxbridge crowded with soldiers
at four o'clock in the morning and had to go round by
way of Berkhamsted to avoid the fighting.

In such circumstances it was wiser not to venture out
at all, and it was only when England had settled down
to a more orderly existence after the Civil War was over
that travellers again began to go about their business
through the country. Some coaches were evidently on
the road by 1655 when Marmaduke Rawdon, a rich
gentleman from Yorkshire, hired a coach-and-six at
Exeter to convey himself and his friends to London.
Quite unexpectedly, while the gentlemen were at breakfast, enjoying their mulled claret before setting off,

'a proper hansome yonge woman' by the name of Mrs
Fax, begged them to take her with them, as she also had
urgent business in London. Rawdon charmingly ac-
quiesced and not only gave her the best seat 'at the
brood end of the coach', but took her up free of charge
and paid all her expenses at the inns along the road,
thereby following, if not inaugurating, a custom which
became familiar to other ladies besides Mrs Fax when
they travelled in the company of gentlemen.

Other coaches, according to Sir Ralph Verney, ran
from London to Winchester and one called the 'Alsberry'
carried some of his visitors down to Claydon. Even so,
only the bravest of travellers could face a journey of any
distance with equanimity, and only a brave adventurer
could have hoped to make a profit out of running a
regular stage-coach from one city to another. Yet in the
summer of 1657, when Oliver Cromwell was within a year
of his death, a coach was started from London to Chester
by a trio of bold speculators, William Dunstan, Henry
Earle and William Fowler.

Chester was a highly important city and, before the
Holyhead route was opened, the main port for Ireland
with a considerable amount of traffic coming and going
through the 'Rows', its famous medieval streets. The
Bear and Billet, once a mansion belonging to the Earls
of Shrewsbury, stood near the Bridge Gate and offered
good entertainment to travellers who were forced to wait
for a favourable wind to carry them across the Irish Sea.
By arrangement with the landlord, the coach from
London arrived there in the late afternoon and set out
again the following morning on the return journey.

It left the George Inn, 'without Aldersgate', every
Monday, Wednesday and Friday and went to Coventry
in two days for 25s., to Stone in three days for 30s. and
to Chester in four days for 35s., and the passengers were
promised that the journey would be 'performed with

much safety, having fresh Horses once a day'. Whether or not this statement really gave them confidence is doubtful. The coach did not keep to its schedule: two years later the same trio of advertisers announced that it was taking five days to reach Chester; none the less their idea of changing the coach horses at the inns along the route as in the post-horse system of travel, was a startling innovation and one that had far-reaching consequences in the future. At this time, fresh horses were harnessed to the coach only when the passengers stopped for their dinner, and each team was fed and rested at night; later, when coach travel had become a fast means of communication, the horses were changed far more frequently at short stages all along the road.

The first travellers on the coach to Chester were also fed and rested at the inns along the road, spending the night in them and starting off again early the next morning. They probably fared less well than the horses, for the inns varied enormously. Accommodation in some of them was not much above the level of the stables. Beds, if they existed, were often verminous and had to be shared with strangers. Travellers, who could not find a bed or afford a big enough tip to the landlord, slept on the floor; or, with their limbs already aching from the cruel jolting of the coach, they dozed upright in a chair. No one, fortunately, thought much about washing: a nip of brandy was more comforting than a basin of water and brandy was only 4d. a glass. It loosened the tongue and revived the spirits of the more timid travellers. After sitting all day cooped up in the coach, they liked each other rather better after supper than before. If the food was edible and the landlord obliging, they could count themselves lucky; if neither came up to their expectations, there was nothing much they could do about it except grumble among themselves when they got back into the coach at dawn the next morning.

2

The six inside passengers sat facing each other on wooden benches with no padding and their feet covered in straw, stout passengers wedging themselves in as best as they could with those of a more slender build. A tall man would find his knees touching the knees of the person opposite to him and his hat, if not his head, in danger of hitting the roof whenever the coach lurched over a bad pot-hole. He was fortunate if he could endure the excessive jolting and swaying of the vehicle without feeling sick, and he could see nothing of the country or of his fellow passengers in wet and chilly weather when the leather curtains were drawn over the unglazed windows and the interior of the coach resembled a damp and draughty box on wheels.

Outside passengers were not taken up on the first coaches—they would at once have been flung off the vehicle owing to the state of the roads; but for a reduced fare, three or four could travel in what was known as 'the conveniency behind', a large wicker-work basket hung on to the back of the coach between the hind wheels by stout leather straps, originally for the purpose of carrying the inside passengers' boxes and bundles of luggage. Anyone suffering from claustrophobia or coach sickness in the fusty, musty smell of damp straw, old leather, unwashed linen and dried sweat inside, might well have been better off in the air outside, except that the boot, or basket, appeared always to be moving sideways like a crab to the general forward motion of the coach and there was no shelter from the elements at all. When a Lancashire clergyman by the name of Edward Parker travelled this way from Preston to London in 1663, he found it intolerable: 'I got to London on Saturday,' he wrote. 'My journey was noe way pleasant, being forced to ride in the boote all the waye. The company yt came up with me were persons of greate qualitie, as knights and ladyes. My journey's expense was 30s. This travell hath soe indisposed mee, yt I am resolved never to ride up againe in ye coatche. I am extremely hott and feverish. What this may tend to I know not. I have not yet advised my doctor.'

What happened to poor Parker when he did advise his doctor is not known; it is to be hoped he went to bed with a hot posset and found some comfort in being between the sheets after such a dreadful experience. In his extremely hot and feverish condition on the journey, he must have mistaken a small-town merchant with his wife or his moll for their betters; for at this time 'persons of greate qualitie' seldom, if ever, even thought of travelling on a public vehicle—it was quite beneath their dignity. Members of the aristocracy travelled in their private coaches and even the country squires owned a chariot of sorts; when making a journey to London they harnessed their shire horses to it, packed their wives and daughters into it and themselves rode on ahead, with a train of servants and country waggons full of luggage in the rear, arriving, much to the amusement of the more sophisticated Londoners, in some disarray.

Pepys bought his own coach from a coachmaker in Cow Lane in 1668. By then he was quite affluent and well on the way to achieving his ambition of being taken for a gentleman. The coach, which was framed but not yet covered in leather when he first saw it, cost £53 and 'being light and very genteel and sober', he was 'mightily pleased with it', though he had to pay out another £50 for a pair of black horses that he bought in Smithfield after a great deal of anxious consultation with his friends. Previously he had always hired a coach, finding the interior darkness of a hackney very convenient for bussing and fondling that merry jade, Mrs Knipp, whenever he escorted her home to her bad-tempered husband. He also hired a travelling coach when he took his wife, her maid, Deb Willet, and his boy, Will Hewer, on an extensive trip to Bath via Oxford, Hungerford and Salisbury, returning through Marlborough, Reading and Maidenhead.

In Oxford he saw some of the Colleges and the Physic Garden, and at Hungerford, 'a mean town', the eels and the crayfish were very good. At Salisbury he lay in 'a silk bed' at the George Inn, but was vexed when he had to pay the bill next day, considering £2 5s. 6d. an exorbitant sum, although it included hiring extra horses for a sight-seeing trip to Stonehenge, where he found the monoliths 'prodigious' and rather frightening. Continuing across Salisbury Plain, he had to hire a guide, for there were no sign-posts of any kind and one of the worst dangers of private travel lay in losing the way on the unfenced roads across the country. Even so, the guide made a mistake and at night, when it was already far too late to be on the road with any comfort, they came to a little inn, where the only guest-room was occupied by a pedlar, fast asleep in a truckle-bed. Having turned him out, they got into his bed and woke up in the morning to find it was 'lowsey', but this, apparently, made them all very merry and they considered themselves extremely lucky not to have spent the night immured in the coach on the bleak and lonely Plain.

They reached Bath the next evening, so weary, Pepys went to bed without any supper, but was up and out early the next morning to take a look at the fine ladies floating in the Cross Bath and was ready to go on to Bristol in the afternoon. Deb Willet's uncle gave them all a handsome feast of venison-pasty, strawberries, 'plenty of brave wine and Bristoll milk' and seemed to be a most 'sober and substantiall merchant'. Then Pepys and his party went back, rather late, 'by moonshine' and a bad road, to Bath, staying there another two nights and leaving on Monday morning, 'without any of the company of the other stage-coaches that go out of this town'—once again alone on the road and in great fear of losing their way over the downs to Marlborough. In fact they saw no other traffic of any kind, only a shepherd or two and the great stones of Avebury standing in a strange hieratic silence under the sky, and they were very glad when they reached the White Hart at Marlborough.

Here, the reckoning for one night was only 14s. 4d. for the entire party, with 2s. for the servants and 1s. extra for the poor, and the next morning they set off again for Newbury, where they dined and heard some music—'a song of the old courtier of Queen Elizabeth's' —before going on to Reading. Will Hewer was 'troubled with the headake' at Reading and Pepys himself was somewhat out of humour all day. The way, however, was 'mighty good from Maydenhead' and they were all very content when they got home to London, except that Mrs Pepys had 'something in her gizzard that only waited an opportunity of being provoked to bring it up'.

2

PERFORMED -IF GOD PERMIT

BY 1667—ONE year before Pepys had made his private journey to Bath—cheaper and faster travel was available to the West of England for those who did not disdain the public coach. Under the dramatic heading FLYING MACHINE, a portentous announcement appeared which said:

> All those desirious to pass from London to Bath, or any other Place on their Road, let them repair to the Bell Savage on Ludgate Hill in London, and the White Lion at Bath, at both which places they may be received in a Stage Coach every Monday, Wednesday and Friday, which performs the Whole Journey in Three Days (if God permit), and sets forth at five o'clock in the morning.
>
> Passengers to pay One Pound five Shillings each, who are allowed to carry fourteen Pounds Weight—for all above to pay three-halfpence per Pound.

While it gave no clue to the proprietors who were bold enough to start a regular coach to Bath, this first advertisement was a sign of the more progressive ideas of the Restoration. By the time it appeared, the bloom was fading a little from the merry England that had welcomed King Charles with garlands of flowers and fountains flowing with wine; some people were shocked by the loose morals of the King and his financial embarrassments. Yet a spirit of optimism and inquiry was in the air and the younger generation, suddenly released from the dreary Puritan régime of no frolic and no fun, enjoyed a new freedom at Court, which set the pace elsewhere. Pleasure was to be found in the most unlikely places and too much indulgence in it cured by a visit to one or the other of the country spas, now beginning to attract the world of fashion.

The one-time Roman city of Bath was not yet the elegant rendezvous it was to become in a later generation dominated by Beau Nash. But those who went there on the advice of Dr Seneschall and Dr Anodyne to plunge into the hot and rather grubby sulphur waters, saw no reason why they should not enjoy some amusement as well, and the city began to expand accordingly, to fill up with quack doctors, apothecaries, musicians, strolling players and mountebanks, all hoping to grow rich out of the idle health seekers and their retinue of attendants. This meant extra traffic on the roads and the success of the 'Flying Machine'. If God did not always permit the journey to be accomplished in three days, that was not the fault of the coach proprietors; their intentions were of the best and were rewarded by an increasing number of travellers. Perhaps Dr Anodyne, who always wore a fur coat in midsummer and is said to have dabbled in magic as well as in medicine, concocting such remedies for the spleen as Burnt Coke quenched in Aqua Vitae or Elks' Hoofs cooked to a cinder—perhaps this learned doctor himself, wrapped in his sables, took the coach from the White Lion to the Bell Savage.

If so, he would have found this famous inn on Ludgate Hill one of the most comfortable in London. It had been in existence ever since the reign of King Henry VI, when it was called the Bell on the Hoop, or Savage's Inn, being the property of a certain John Savage, who made it and all its appurtenances over to his widowed mother in 1453. In the days of Queen Elizabeth I, plays were acted in the yard and later, a performing horse called Marocco was exhibited to a crowd of spectators by a Scotsman named Banks. Wrestling, cock-fighting, bear-baiting and gambling of all sorts went on there, with the lusty, fractious mob of London apprentices often in a dangerous humour. But now, the yard, entered through an archway on the north side of Ludgate Hill, had become a busy centre for the coaching activity of the new age.

Travellers arriving or setting out were well catered for. On the ground floor there was a dining-room and a tap-room, and the yard was surrounded by three tiers of galleries giving access to the bedrooms. Only the very best of the inns in the City could boast as the Bell Savage did of '40 rooms with good Cellarage, Stabling for 100 Horses and other Good Accommodations', though exactly what these other accommodations were is a matter for conjecture. 'A very Strange Beast called a RHYNOCEROS, lately brought over from the East Indies, being the *first that ever was in England*' was to be seen there daily in 1684 from nine in the morning until eight at night, and was certainly a curiosity for any travellers who came up from Bath and found their journey ending in a meeting with this unlovely beast. Another and more charming attraction for them was the pot of flowers hanging near the archway, which shook surprisingly as the coaches swept past it, for this was

carved by Grinling Gibbons and the first of his works
to be noticed by John Evelyn, who thereupon recom-
mended the master wood-carver to Charles II.

Whether or not the King himself ever stepped into the
yard of the Bell Savage to admire the Gibbons carving,
the landlord, whose name was Henry Young, must
have found the fortuitous connexion with royalty
exceedingly good for business. To run a large inn
successfully he needed to be a person of some consequence, able to exercise control over his staff of stable-
boys, ostlers, cooks, chamber-maids and waiters, besides
having to provide enough food for human consumption
and enough fodder for the horses. He had to know how
to keep accurate accounts and above all, how to differen-
tiate between his customers. If he owned the Bath coach
or had some financial interest in it, he would have treated
the passengers with considerable goodwill, though not
with the degree of obsequiousness he would have reserved
for persons of quality travelling in private. He would
also have charged them according to their rank in
society, not from any personal sentiments of greed or
snobbery, simply because the line dividing the gentry
from the rest of the population was so firmly drawn no
one could ignore it. For some of his regulars he issued a
token with his own sign engraved on it, which he took
in payment for the services he rendered. 'All persons
who had any Accompts with him or Farthings belonging
to the Said House' were able to change them back into
the usual currency when the Great Plague paralysed
the whole of London in the summer of 1665 and the
Bell Savage was shut down, but this somewhat complicated system of payment continued for many years after
the inn reopened.

The Bath coach from the Bell Savage was not the only
one to be called a 'Flying Machine'. There was a 'Flying
Coach' to Oxford, which did the fifty-five mile journey

from London in one day, the fastest time yet known, and for the modest sum of 12s., later reduced to 10s. Being much cheaper and a great improvement on the earlier Oxford coach which had taken two days with a night at Beaconsfield, it naturally became extremely popular with students of the University, who took a chance on riding up to the capital for a lark or a night out and were able to return the next day before college discipline caught up with them. Oxford, according to Pepys, was 'a very sweet place and well seated', with cheap entertainment and wonderful strawberries at 1s. 2d.—well worth a day's journey, even if it meant leaving London at six in the morning and not arriving until seven in the evening. The road through Uxbridge, Beaconsfield and High Wycombe was better than some of the other roads in the kingdom, because Charles II had a hunting lodge at Woodstock and to facilitate his coming and going with pretty witty Nellie Gwyn or the mistress most in favour at any given moment, the road had to be kept in reasonable repair.

Elsewhere the roads were patched by the villagers, who resented the work exceedingly and either did nothing about it, or attacked the unfortunate, unpaid road surveyors appointed by each parish to look into the matter, with stones and scythes and pitchforks or any other implement they could lay hands on. Some attempt was made in the reign of Charles II to introduce a more organized system of turnpikes or toll-gates, whereby travellers paying a fee to pass each gate were supposed to be contributing to a general fund for keeping the roads in repair; but the tolls were farmed out to various persons of doubtful integrity, who lined their own pockets whenever they saw an opportunity of doing so instead of putting the money into the fund, and the roads remained much the same—dangerous, difficult and in winter virtually impassable.

Danger lay hidden everwhere, and the fear of robbery and violence continued to distress everyone who travelled except certain ladies of rank and fashion who found the highwaymen romantic and exciting. One young lady was said to have danced a *coranto* on Hounslow Heath with 'the first Gentleman of the Road', Claude Duval, while her husband sat waiting in the coach, and hundreds of others went into mourning when Duval was eventually caught and hanged at Tyburn in 1670. The glamour attached to a few of these gay and gallant gentleman of the road did not, however, minimize the risk. Hounslow, Finchley and the Surrey commons were places of terror for the ordinary traveller, liable at any moment to be held up by a tough, hard-riding, belligerent rascal with his face hidden by a *crêpe* mask and a pair of horse-pistols which meant business and were not just pointed at the traveller's head for fun. With luck the robber might take no more than the traveller's purse or his watch, though many a victim who had thoughtfully stuffed his gold into his boots or sewn it up in the lining of his breeches, was stripped and left to the mercies of the next Good Samaritan coming down the road. Nothing and no one was safe; and the grizzly idea of hanging the dead bodies of the highwaymen from gibbets at various points along the road, instead of acting as a deterrent to the gangs still at large, only served to terrify the travellers all the more.

Very little of the loot the thieves ran off with was ever recovered. Newspapers were full of advertisements similar to the one printed in the *London Gazette* in 1684, which said: 'A GENTLEMAN (passing with others in the Northampton Stage Coach on Wednesday the 14th instant, by Harding Common about two miles from Market Street) was set upon by four Theeves, plain in habit but well-horsed, and there (amongst other things) robbed of a Watch; the description of it thus; The

Maker's Name was engraven on the Back plate in French,
Gulimus Petit à Londres; it was of a large round Figure,
flat, Gold Enamelled without, with a variety of flowers
of different colours and within a Landskip, and by a fall
the Enamel was a little cracked; it had also a black
Seale-Skin plain case lined with Green Velvet.' The
owner was offering a reward of one guinea to anyone
returning this gem of a watch to Mr Samuel Gibbs,
Saddler, near the George Inn, Northampton, or to Mr
Cross in Wood Street, London, but it is very doubtful
whether he ever saw it or the little 'landskip' within
again.

Some of the innkeepers along the road were in league
with the highwaymen and tipped them off when rich
travellers stopped to bait their horses or to stay a night
on their premises. At the Bell, Hounslow, the landlord
devised an elaborate system of passing the information
on and it was a long time before the law caught up with
him. Authority was slow and the highwaymen were
fast. The traveller's only hope was to trust no one and
to defend himself at the crucial moment or, if he valued
his skin more than his property, to part with his gold
without a fight. Some lost their money and their lives,
for according to Sir John Verney, who was staying in
London in June 1698, 'Six forraigners goeing for France
were robb'd in the Dover Stage Coach at Shooter's Hill
and lost about 300 pound, one of them Kill'd by the
Rogues who got off with the prize . . . Severall other
Roberies have been lately committed on the Roads
about this Towne,' he added, 'soe that it is very dangerous travelling at present,' and for him to get back to
Claydon where he had succeeded his father as Lord of the
Manor, was no small undertaking. He sent his 'night-
gowne' ahead in a locked box—a strange thing to do if he
only had one—and himself took the public coach to
Aylesbury, instructing his agent to meet him there with

two horses, so that he could ride home the same night if he was not already too exhausted by the 'dirty wayes' and the nervous strain of the journey.

Yet in spite of the perils of travelling, the stage-coaches were gradually becoming more popular. The pioneers of the Chester coach at the George Inn, without Aldersgate, were now advertising coaches to several parts of Britain: to Salisbury in two days, Blandford and Dorchester in two and a half, and to Axminster and Exeter in four days; to Stamford, Newark, Doncaster and York; to 'Ockington and Plimouth', Birmingham, Wolverhampton and Shrewsbury, and to Edinburgh, 'once a fortnight for £4 apeece'. The George Inn had grown in size and in importance, with 'a very commodious Place-Chamber and Outhouses, Stables, Yards, Riding Place and Garden with other Conveniencies', and when the coaches were packing up to go out, the yard was a scene of frantic activity. Ostlers and stable-boys, occupied in harnessing the horses, had little time to spare for the passengers, bewildered by the chances of stepping into the wrong coach and finding themselves on the way to Shrewsbury instead of Salisbury. The booking-office was still a makeshift cubby-hole screened off from the hall and manned by a sleepy boot-boy or by the innkeeper himself when he was not too busy elsewhere running after his guests. Some passengers waited along the road at some distance from the inn, having bribed the coachman to pick them up for less than the proper fare, the money going into the coachman's pocket instead of into the innkeeper's. But for those who had spent the night at the George, breakfast was a hurried affair, gobbled in the pale light of the morning, with time perhaps for a mutton chop and a glass of ale, nothing more, and the thought of a long, long journey ahead. Luggage was bundled up into bags and baskets that were quite inadequate and might easily end up in Salisbury

instead of in Shrewsbury if not watched with care, and
the passengers themselves surveyed each other with some
misgivings. Going on a journey was, indeed, an adventure
or an anxiety, according to the way each individual happened to look at it. Some made their wills before setting
out, others said their prayers and hoped God would permit them to arrive intact at their destination.

Ralph Thoresby of Leeds, a pious and God-fearing
antiquary, who travelled the country on horseback in
search of curios for his 'Museum of Rarities', thought he
would try the coach for a change, but was 'fearful of
being confined for so many days with unsuitable persons
and not one I know of'. He had to ride from Leeds to
York as there was no coach service between the two in
1683, and to spend the night at the Black Swan to be up
in time in the morning to begin his journey to London.
At this season of the year—in February—the coach took
six days to reach the capital, through Ferrybridge, Doncaster, Newark and Stamford, all down the Great North
Road, where the highwaymen lurked in panther-like
secrecy, waiting to pounce on their victims. Witham
Common, near Stamford, where a friend of Thoresby's
had once killed a vicious rogue, was a desolate waste of
land and the quicker the coach could get across it the
better for his peace of mind. No wonder he wrote, on
arriving safely at the Black Swan in Holborn: 'God be
thanked for his mercies to me and my poor family.'

Yet Thoresby evidently found coach travel a convenient way of getting around the country. It saved the
wear and tear on his clothes compared with riding on
horseback in all weathers, and since there was more safety
in numbers than in being alone, he could, if he dared,
leave his pistols at home, while he need not burden himself with an extra suit and a new hat; he could go into the
coach wearing an embroidered waistcoat, silk stockings
or an 'Indian gown with a sash', without fear of them

being ruined when he arrived. And ladies could travel in whatever frills or finery they chose. For them coaches were a great improvement on riding pillion behind their husbands or a servant and quite a number, like Mrs Fax, travelled alone without friends or relations to support them, though the perils of the road must have frightened them exceedingly and any journey they undertook demanded courage and endurance, if only to withstand the vagaries of the English climate changing from the extreme cold of a windowless coach on a windy day to the suffocating heat and dust of the summer. Fortunately, never having striven for equality with the male

A seventeenth-century coach from Loggan's Oxonia Illustrata, *1674*
JOHN R. FREEMAN

sex, they expected—and received—a kindness and a civility which constantly helped them on their way. Gentlemen took care to protect them; Ralph Thoresby was no less gallant towards them than Marmaduke Rawdon. On one of his later journeys from York to London, he and his fellow passengers paid for their refreshments. 'Between Grantham and Stamford they were more chargeable with wine and brandy than the former part of the journey, wherein we had neither,' he commented—but perhaps he thought the ladies had gone

a bit too far, for 'the next day,' he added, 'we gave them
leave to treat themselves.'

At the Black Swan in Holborn they would all have
been well entertained. This, with the Bell, the Black Bull
and the George and Blue Boar, was one of the four great
inns built by Sir Kenelm Digby after the Restoration to
recover the fortune he had lost in the Civil War, and as
London began to eat up the fields of Clerkenwell,
Bloomsbury and Soho, in a strategic position to serve
the growing number of coach travellers arriving from the
north. Moreover, Ralph Thoresby and the ladies from
Grantham, if they were in luck, had only to look out of
the windows of the Black Swan to get a thrill as eye-
witnesses of an event they could talk about when they
got home to their provincial cities, for the carts bearing
criminals from Newgate to the gallows at Tyburn passed
regularly along Holborn. Some of them stopped at the
George and Blue Boar, where the convicted men—or
women—if they were of sufficient importance, were given
one last tot of brandy before they reached their hideous
end. A mob of jeering, stinking and shouting citizens
surrounded them, following the carts on their dreary way
to watch one more man—or woman—brought to justice
and their still-warm human entrails exposed to the gaping
populace; and Ralph Thoresby, kind-hearted though he
was, believed it was right and proper and the will of God.

Coaches, bound for the west and south-west of England,
also passed along Holborn to Tyburn before going on
through the rich county of Middlesex. One called the
'Highflyer' had set off from the Rose, a smaller inn by
the bridge over the River Fleet, as early as 1648, with
the water-poet, John Taylor, and some friends of his who
were bound for the Isle of Wight to see the captive
Charles I, their 'gracious Soveraigne, afflicted Lord and
Master', imprisoned in Carisbrooke Castle. In spite of the
melancholy occasion of their journey, they enjoyed them-

selves immensely; for Taylor, by then a man of sixty-eight, with an adventurous career behind him as a sailor in Queen Elizabeth's triumphant wooden ships, a Thames waterman, a Yeoman of the Guard and a wag, was a rollicking companion and game for anything. With his astonishing vigour and his usual aplomb, he recorded the incidents of his trip in verse:

We took our coach, two coachmen and four horses,
And merrily from London made our courses.
We wheel'd the top of th' heavy hill call'd Holborne
(Up which hath been full many a sinful soule borne),
And so along we jolted past St Gileses,
Which place from Brainford six (or neare) seven
    miles is.
To Stanes that night at five o'clock we coasted,
Where (at the Bush) we had bak'd, boyl'd and
    roasted.
Bright Sol's illustrious Rayes the day adorning,
We past Bagshot and Bawwaw Friday morning.
That night we lodged at the White Hart at Alton,
And had good meate—a table with a salt on.
Next morn w'arose with blushing cheek'd Aurora;
The wayes were faire, but not so faire as Flora,
For Flora was a goddesse, and a woman,
And (like the highwayes) to all men was common.
Our Horses, with the Coach, which we went into,
Did hurry us amaine, through thick and thine too;
With fiery speed, the foaming bit they champt on,
And brought us to the Dolphin at Southampton.

Eighty miles in three days was not bad going in the month of October, and it is to be hoped that the cheerful water-poet and his friends brought some comfort to their sad and pale-faced King, even if they had to suppress the 'faire wayes' of Flora at the White Hart in Alton. Taylor

3

himself ended up as an innkeeper, becoming the landlord of the Crown in Phoenix Alley off Long Acre and, with a fine flourish of loyalty after the King was executed, changing his sign to the Mourning Crown in defiance of Cromwell's secret police.

Nothing more is heard of the Southampton 'Highflyer' after Taylor's journey, though coaches were running to far more distant parts of the south and south-west by the end of the seventeenth century. They went to Blandford and Dorchester, to Bridport, Axminster, Honiton and Exeter; and at Axminster, when John Gay went there, he encountered not only another Flora who washed his shirt for him and sent him to bed in her own smock, but an expert female barber, who wore a heavy gold chain round her neck and three gold rings on her 'easy fingers', which moved so smoothly over his chin, he thought they were 'as soft as when Venus strok'd the beard of Jove'. Some travellers evidently were beginning to take pleasure in their journeys and the facilities offered to them down the road were improving.

3

INNS ALONG THE ROAD

'THE WORLD AFFOORDS not such Innes as England hath, either for good and cheap entertainment after the Guests owne pleasure, or for humble attendance on the Passengers,' wrote one satisfied traveller, admiring 'the variety of the meates, the curtesie of the Host and Hostesse ... and the Musitians, who offered to give himm the good day with musicke in the morning'. But it was not always so. Another traveller—a lady—wrote of one of the inns at Knaresborough: 'This house and all that is in it is horribly nasty and crowded up with all sorte of company, which we Eate with in a roome as the spiders are redy to drope into my mouthe, and sure hath nethor been well cleaned nor ared this doseven yerese'—a horrifying picture of what travellers in the seventeenth century might have to put up with on their journeys, though possibly an exception to the more general rule of good entertainment.

For innkeepers and their wives—many of the former, ex-soldiers, who rejoiced in the restoration of the monarchy and were royalists to a man—were beginning to see a profit in welcoming their guests with good accomodation and good food. Beds had improved enormously,

25

being furnished with flock or feather mattresses, bolsters
and pillows, and sometimes, as Pepys had discovered in
Salisbury, hung with silk curtains or tapestries which
made them warm and cosy to sleep in. Admittedly they
were still over-crowded and had to be shared—especially
if the judges were holding Assize courts in the neighbourhood or when there was an election, a prize-fight or some
horse-racing going on—and it was not surprising that
Ralph Thoresby found it difficult to get enough privacy
to say his prayers in comfort; but clean sheets, 'wherein
no man hath been lodged since they came from the laun-
dress or out of the water wherein they were last washed',
were often available and clean napery at the dining-table
was considered a necessity, since there were very few
forks in use and people had the habit of wiping their fingers on the table-cloth.

Personal cleanliness was more difficult to come by. Hot
and dusty travellers could not have taken a bath even if
they had thought of doing so, which was most unlikely.
Pepys caught a cold having his ears washed, and recorded
the rare occasions when he reluctantly cleaned himself
with warm water—to please his wife, because she did the
same. Such ablutions were performed in the kitchen over
a basin; plumbing was virtually unknown. A closet on
the lines invented by Queen Elizabeth I's godson, Sir
John Harington, was located in the house of office somewhere in the cellar or the back garden; otherwise guests
at the inns were provided with chamber-pots, which were
the source of a great many obscene jokes and any amount
of indecent horseplay. The wise traveller, whether a
gentleman or a lady, carried a nosegay of sweet-smelling
flowers and herbs, and smoking also helped to palliate a
too sensitive nose, though non-smokers objected strongly
to the pungent odours of black Virginia tobacco.

Lady Elmes—a sister of Sir Ralph Verney and the lady
who had been shocked by the spiders at Knaresborough

—complained of another sort of smell and of lacking the means to rectify it when she was staying at Astrop Wells, a watering-place in Northamptonshire. 'Instead of the sweet woodbines and jessamine att Claydon,' she wrote to her brother, 'I have the stincke of sower whay and cheese, which is so strong in my chamber I know not what to doe . . . not a coale of fyer can I get to burne one smale bitt of perfewme.' In fact, the service at this particular inn seems to have been non-existent and poor Lady Elmes was at her wits' end. 'Fast I must at night,' she continued, 'heare not being athor master or maid att home, and candle there is not a bit, soe I have sent to borrow one. . . .' Once again, what with the smell of cheese, nothing for supper and no lighting or heating, Lady Elmes was evidently very unlucky in her choice of somewhere to stay—or was she too fussy and too eager to find fault?

As a rule the innkeepers and their wives still gave a great deal more of their attention to individual travellers than to the passengers on the coach, for the simple reason that it was in the nature of their business to do so. The individual travellers hired a private room and com-manded their dinner or their supper to be brought to them while they warmed their toes in front of the fire, the host and hostess considering it a great honour if they were allowed to sit for a while at the table to drink a glass of wine with them. They paid extra for these additional comforts and for wax candles to light the room, and the servants attending them expected a generous tip the next morning. Coach passengers were less affluent; although they could also hire a private room if they wished, they usually dined at the common table in the parlour, or in the kitchen, where they had some advantage in being able to watch their food being cooked and 'the meate dressed' in the way they preferred.

The English were enormous meat eaters at all times

and travelling increased their appetite. Beef and mutton were the staple dishes, whether in large joints roasted or boiled, or cut into rump steaks and juicy chops. Plenty of poultry and game also appeared on the dining-table: peacocks, swans and goose at the larger inns, ducks, capons, woodcock, wheatears, larks and even swallows in the summer; and of all nations and countries, England had always been 'the best served of fish, not only of all manner of sea-fish, but also of fresh-water fish and of all manner of sorts of salt-fish'.

There were a dozen ways of cooking eels: spitchcocked, smoked, *water-souché*, stewed, fried, boiled and baked among them; and since perishable foods could not be quickly and easily transported over the bad roads, each district had its own speciality, giving the traveller a wonderful variety of choice as he journeyed through the country. Cambridge was famous for its brawn, Newbury for its crayfish, Kent for its huffkins and Melton Mowbray for its pies. There were ducks and apple sauce at Aylesbury, pink lobsters and crabs at Morecambe, venison pies and pasties in Chester, pigeons and pork in Birmingham and ham at York. Cheddar cheese, Wensleydale, Double Gloucester and Stilton could only be found where they belonged, but gooseberry-pie, gooseberry-fool and plum pudding appeared almost everywhere. Ralph Thoresby never stopped at Grantham without buying the special cakes that were made there, called Grantham Whetstones, and other travellers relished the famous cakes of Shrewsbury and Banbury and the buns in Bath. England was a paradise for the gourmet and her cooks had never been better.

No one drank water—it was hard to obtain and often unwholesome. In cities like Chester it was carried up from the river in leather bags; in the country it had to be drawn from the nearest well. Men, women and children drank ale instead and thrived on it. Most of the innkeepers brewed their own and it varied with the local water, so that Yorkshire ale was much stronger than any other. Different inns specialized in their own particular brew: buttered ale was warmed and flavoured with sugar, cinnamon and butter; mum was brewed with wheat instead of hops and lamb's wool mixed with the pulp of apples. All three could be extremely potent—and so could cider, which became a favourite drink in the West Country and especially in Worcestershire, where Lord Scudamore of Holme Lacy brought his famous Redstreak cider to perfection. Metheglin, a mead made from fermented honey, elderberry and gooseberry wines were a homely substitute for the more expensive foreign wines imported from the Continent, though many of the innkeepers kept a store of claret, sherry and port in their cellars and the habit of drinking brandy, brought home by the English sailors from the Dutch Wars, was spreading like wildfire through the land.

Coach passengers really needed these 'strong waters' after the shaking they got on the road, though how many of them after feeling sick all the way down the Exeter Road, were actually revived or made to feel more bilious at Honiton by the landlady's sillabubs of sweet wine mixed with cream, is a matter for speculation. She meant well, whatever the result, and was known as one of the most motherly hostesses to be met with on the road, in contrast to the handsome, rakish kind, who could only 'dress fine and entertain the soldiers, be free with their favours and calculating when it came to being paid for them'. Complaints, of course, were made about the merrymaking at the inns by the more puritan-minded section of the population; but the innkeepers and many of their wives, too, were of a convivial disposition—they had to be—and their status in the community was fairly high. The parlour and the tap-room were the chief centres of news in the country towns and villages. Visitors from

abroad were astonished to discover how easily and
naturally the gentry mixed with the farmers and the
labourers in their snug and cosy surroundings. Here the
price of corn was discussed, the points of the squire's
new horse weighed up, the judgement of the village
parson or the justice of the peace considered, and the
weather, more often than not, condemned; while travellers, arriving from afar, were encouraged to talk on the
state of the world beyond the parish boundaries.

Unhappily for the travellers, coaches were not improving so quickly as the inns down the road. Pepys reported
that a 'glass-coach', with velvet cushions, had been
designed for the Duke of York in 1661, and five years
later, he watched some of Colonel Blount's experiments
in St George's Fields, without thinking very highly of
them. Indeed, to find a way of constructing any springs
strong enough to stand up to the condition of the roads,
defeated almost everyone—even Obadiah Elliot, a coachmaker in Lambeth, who was awarded the Gold Medal of
the Royal Society of Arts for his 'new, patent elliptical
springs'. In theory, his new springs, highly commended
by the Worshipful Company of Coach Builders and
Harness Makers, were excellent; in practice they just did
not work at all, and they were only fitted to a few private
chariots, not to any of the public coaches. Travellers in
these still had to put up with being thrown backwards
and forwards or sideways, as they rattled on to their
destination.

Not everyone welcomed the new form of transport. In
London, the Thames watermen complained loudly:

Carroches, coaches, jades and Flanders mares,
Doe rob us of our shares, our wares, our fares;
Against the ground we stand and knock our heels
Whilst all our profit runs away on wheels . . . .

And this was perfectly true—the watermen could not compete with the new surge of traffic in the streets; by 1699, when there were eight hundred hackney coaches for hire, they were a dying community, their boats lying idle on the water and their furious fighting for a likely customer of no avail.

The sedan-chairmen were luckier. They carried people of rank and fashion on short distances through the city from the middle of the seventeenth century until the beginning of the nineteenth and were an indispensable feature of town life, though a quarrelsome, grasping, ill-mannered set of Cockney and Irish roughs, always fighting each other and spying on the people they took up. Many a young lady lost her reputation through the gossip of the chairmen carrying her to an assignation and in the eyes of some moralists, the sedan-chair and sin were fatally coupled together.

But the moralists also attacked coaching. John Cresset, who lived in the Charterhouse, was particularly vitriolic in his condemnation of the new form of transport and wrote a long pamphlet on the subject, suggesting that coaches ought to be suppressed altogether. According to his view: 'These stage Coaches make Gentlemen come to London on every small occasion, which otherwise they would not do but upon Necessity; nay, the convenience of the Passage makes their wives often come up, who, rather than come such long journeys on horseback, would stay at home. Then when they come to Town they must presently be in the Mode, get fine Cloathes, go to Plays and Treats, and, by these means, get such a Habit of Idleness and Love of Pleasure as makes them uneasie ever after.'

Like most moralists before or since, Cresset was badly overstating his case. Many wives, devoted to their husbands, suffered extremely from the long separations they often had to endure by staying at home when it was

impracticable for them to go to town. With only the servants and their children for company in some isolated
manor house in the depths of the country, who could
blame them if they moped a bit and longed for a little
frivolity now and again? Lady Verney worried about her
husband's health when he was called away to the House
of Commons and, when she joined him in London, bought
a lot of things like 'sope and oil', which she could not get
at Claydon. Besides, there were tantalizing shops in
Covent Garden and the Strand, milliners and mantua-
makers in Jermyn Street, ribbon-vendors and sellers of
fancy goods, shoes, French gloves, stockings and satin
petticoats trimmed with silver lace—things that were
never seen in the shires; and even the most frivolous
wives, when not too busy about their own affairs, may
well have found it convenient to keep an eye on their husbands, whose business in town would not have been
unmixed with pleasure.

Cresset, however, was equally strong in condemning
his own sex when they forsook the manly custom of
riding a horse for sitting in a coach. 'Travelling in these
Coaches can neither prove advantageous to Man's health
or business,' he wrote. 'For what advantage is it to Man's
health to be called out of their Beds into these Coaches
an hour before day in the morning, to be hurried in them
from place to place till one, two or three hours within
night; insomuch that after sitting all day in the summer-
time stifled with heat and choked with dust; or in the
Winter time, starving or freezing with cold, or choked
with filthy Fogs, they are often brought to their Inns by
Torchlight, when it is too late to sit up to get a Supper;
and next morning they are forced into the coach so early,
that they can get no breakfast?'

This hardly sounds like 'the convenient passage'
Cresset was thinking of earlier on, but there was worse
to come: 'What addition is this to mens Health or Busi-

ness, to ride all day with strangers, oftentimes sick, ancient, deseased Persons, or young Children crying; to whose humours they are obliged to be subject, forced to bear with, and many times are poisoned with their nasty scents, and cripled by the crowd of their Boxes and Bundles? Is it for a Man's Health to travel with tired Jades, to be laid fast in the foul Wayes, and forced to wade up to the knees in mire; afterwards to sit in the cold till Teams of Horses can be sent to pull the Coach out?'

No one, apparently, answered Cresset's pertinent questions in the affirmative; no one took much notice of him, except to wonder if he had some ulterior motive in wanting to kill the coaching business. Men, accustomed to riding long distances, did not at once become 'infirm of purpose, soft and grievously enervated' as he had prophesied, and women—well, perhaps Jeremiah Cresset did not know that most women only listen to what they want to hear.

Another writer supported Cresset on the strange grounds that if coaches were suppressed, more wine and beer would be drunk at the inns to the great increase and advantage of the Excise revenue, but the public did not heed him either, in spite of his curious reason for inviting everyone to take to the bottle. By 1681, according to De Laune's *Survey of London*, there were one hundred and nineteen coaches running from the capital city, between sixty and seventy of them long-distance conveyances and the remainder serving places up to twenty-five miles away. There were seven coaches to Windsor, six of them going out and coming in daily; five to Bath and Bristol, the second largest city in the kingdom; four to Exeter, three to Guildford, and two to Cambridge, Canterbury, Chelmsford, Gloucester, Lincoln and Stamford, Norwich, Oxford, Portsmouth, Reading, Saffron-Walden and Ware. Between London and York, Chester and Exeter, more than fifty passengers a week were travelling in the high season between Easter and Michaelmas. Coach

travel could not, in fact, be suppressed, any more than
Canute could command the sea to withdraw: it had
become a part of the English scene.

Edward Chamberlayne, who published a book every
year called *The Present State of Great Britain*, wrote in
his edition for 1684: 'There is of late such an admirable
commodiousness for both men and women to travel from
London to the principal towns in the country, that the
like hath not been known in the world; and that is by
stage-coaches, wherein anyone may be transported to any
place, sheltered from foul weather and foul ways, free
from endamaging of one's health and one's body by hard
jogging or over-violent motion, and this not only at the
low price of about a shilling for every five miles, but with
such velocity and speed in one hour as that the post in
some foreign countries cannot make in one day.'

Chamberlayne was a patriot. For him the nasty scents
and the fretful children, the tired jades and the boxes and
bundles which Cresset found so offensive, were of no
importance. He was proud of Britain's coaching service
and marvelled at it. The only thing he could not know
was how it would develop in the next century.

NOTICE.

This Coach leaves London at Six o'clock in the Morning.

From the George and Blue Boar, Holborn.

4

TURNPIKES AND TRAFFIC

PROGRESS WAS SLOW at the beginning of the eighteenth century. Coaches were still heavy, lumbering vehicles covered in dull black leather and studded with numerous broad-headed nails. The window frames, painted red, were still hung with dingy leather curtains and the interior was dark and smelly. The seats still had no cushions, and the 'conveniency behind', more aptly nick-named the 'rumble-tumble', was as bad as it had ever been. Anyone brave enough to occupy it at half-price soon discovered how much he would have to suffer before his journey ended, sitting up to his knees in straw, but with no other sort of padding at all to protect him.

Six stout horses with strong muscle-power were still needed to draw the clumsy stage-coaches along the agonizing roads, with all the inconvenience and danger of the whole outfit being overturned or breaking down. And at this time, royalty fared no better than the public —in fact, rather worse, for the richly carved embellishments, the gilded cupids and the tritons that decorated the royal coach, only added extra weight to it. When Queen Anne, suffering one of her acute attacks of gout, decided to remove her Court from Windsor to Bath, it

took her four days to get there. Eight waggons carrying
her officers in attendance followed the royal coach and a
ninth was put at the disposal of the Queen's dearest
friend, the Duchess of Marlborough, who was, perhaps,
already in a bad temper with her royal mistress, since she
made the journey 'with the blinds drawn'.

Fortunately the mayor and the other civic dignitaries,
who welcomed Her Majesty with loyal addresses and
pealing bells, had considered carefully the immense
weight of the royal coach carrying the somewhat heavy
royal lady in relation to the contours of the city of Bath,
and the near disaster which had attended the Queen's
previous visit as Princess Anne, was avoided. On that
occasion, while ascending the steep Lansdown Hill, the
company had watched with horror and amazement as the
horses of the Princess's coach, unable to go any farther,
had suddenly stopped and straddled their legs in a vain
attempt to keep their royal cargo from rolling backwards
down the hill. Only by the quick action of a dozen or more
lusty footmen and loyal Somersetshire yeomen, who
rushed to the rear end of the coach and made a human
wall against its backward progress down the hill, was the
future Queen saved from a serious accident—and even so
she was extremely shaken.

Her dull husband, Prince George of Denmark, had an
equally unhappy experience in 1702, when travelling
from Windsor to Petworth in Sussex to meet the King of
Spain, who was on a state visit to Britain and had arrived
at Portsmouth two days earlier. One of the Prince's
attendants described how they set out from Windsor at
six in the morning by torchlight and did not get out of
their coaches, 'save only when they were overturned or
stuck fast in the mire', till they arrived at their journey's
end. ''Twas hard service for the Prince,' he wrote, 'to sit
fourteen hours in a coach that day without eating anything and passing through the worst ways I ever saw in

my life. We were thrown but once indeed in going, but our coach which was the leading one, and his Highness's body coach would have suffered much if the nimble boors of Sussex had not frequently poised it or supported it with their shoulders from Godalming almost to Petworth; and the nearer we approached the Duke of Somerset's house, the more inaccessible it seemed to be. The last nine miles of the way cost us about six hours to conquer them; and indeed we had never done it if our good master had not, several times, lent us a pair of horses out of his own coaching whereby we were able to trace out a road for him.'

Why the Prince was not properly provided by the royal kitchens with at least a leg of cold chicken to nibble on his journey, cannot now be said—and how the King of Spain fared coming in the other direction from Portsmouth to Petworth, is not known; if he, too, had to be supported by the nimble boors of Sussex, their dialect mixed with the passionate expletives of his nervous Spanish entourage must have caused considerable confusion, but perhaps the roads in England were no worse than those in Spain.

Queen Anne's ministers were somewhat slow in realizing that it was time something should be done about the roads; they concentrated more on deepening the rivers and making them navigable for the increasing amount of goods traffic passing from the country to London. Then, in a sudden burst of energy, twelve new Turnpike Acts were passed through Parliament, authorizing toll-gates to be set up every five miles or so along some of the main routes, the charges varying from one region to another, being most expensive on the roads leading out of London. Horsemen paid 1d. to pass each gate, coaches 1s. 6d., carts or carriages with two horses 4¼d., and drovers 5d. for a score of oxen and 2d. for a score of pigs, if they could not manage, as they usually did, to dodge

the toll-gates altogether by picking their way round
them.

Most travellers resented being stopped and having to
pay the surly turnpike-men, who lived in picturesque
little round houses beside the gates; yet the system was
the only one that began to make some difference to the
roads, and one of its most enthusiastic supporters was
Daniel Defoe. Journeying about the country as the secret
agent of Robert Harley, the Tory leader, and collecting
material for his *Tour Through England and Wales*, published some ten years later, Defoe had good reason to be
grateful for the improvements he found. Travelling sometimes on horseback and sometimes by stage-coach, his
knowledge of England and the English roads was second
to none. He marvelled at the remaining stretch of the
Fosse Way, which was still as sound as when the Romans
had built it and he actually saw a section of it cut into by
an intelligent surveyor who was trying to discover how
so durable a road had ever been constructed. 'But now
labour is dear,' he reflected, 'wages are high and no man
works for bread and water . . . so that rich as we are, it
would exhaust the whole nation to build the causeways
which the Romans built with very little expence'—a
sobering thought for one who had so much faith in his
own generation. Yet Defoe never lost heart and his
observations, based on his own personal experience of
what was happening all around him, fortified his natural
optimism. With the same meticulous passion for detail
that he had shown in his already famous *Robinson
Crusoe*, he noted the variations on the different roads in
the kingdom: why in the deep clays of the Midland
counties they were more difficult to keep in repair, how
the continual treading of the heavy bullocks and other
beasts being driven into London to Smithfield Market
wore away the surface and how the traveller was constantly annoyed by having to wade through 'the smaller

waters, oftentimes the most dangerous to travellers on hasty rains and always most injurious to the roads by lying in holes and puddles, to the great spoiling of the bottom and making constant sloughs, sometimes able to bury both man and horse'.

Out of the turnpike funds, when properly administered, some of these evils were overcome. 'We now see the most dismal piece of ground that ever was in England, handsomely repaired,' Defoe reported, referring to the great north-west road to Chester and its offshoot running from the top of the chalky hill beyond Dunstable Down to Hockley, 'justly called Hockley in the Hole', and on to Newport Pagnell and Northampton. Then there was the great highway from London through Essex to Ipswich and Harwich, 'the most worn with waggons, carts and carriages and with droves of black cattle, hogs and sheep of any road in England', now, as a result of the turnpikes set up at the corner of Dog Row near Mile End and at Romford, 'so firm, so safe, so easy to travellers and carriages as well as cattle' that few roads in the country could equal it.

New bridges were built over the rivers and the smaller waters, one mile of the road between two new bridges south of Streatham costing the alarming sum of £1,000; but Defoe believed quite rightly, that 'no publick edifice, almshouse, hospital or nobleman's palace could be of equal value to the country or more of an honour and an ornament to it' than the road-building he saw going on about him. Not only would travellers benefit from it: 'the fat cattle will drive lighter and come to market with less toil and consequently both go farther in one day and not waste their flesh and heat and spoil themselves in wallowing through the sloughs and the mud as is now the case'.

Drovers were supposed to give way to coaches and carriages, though this unwritten law of the road was not

4

always observed, and to be caught up in a herd of black
bullocks on the way through Islington added to the
travellers' discomforts and caused intolerable delays.
Coachmen, not in the best of tempers and full of too
much drink, lashed about them with their whips, cursing
loudly, much to the consternation of any ladies sitting in
the coach, who were powerless to do anything about it.
Few passengers, indeed, ever dared to interfere with the
coachman—had they done so, they would have been sure
to get the worst of any argument; for the coachmen were
a tough, hard-fighting, hard-drinking set of men, inured
to all kinds of weather and not over-sensitive about the
way they treated their 'cattle' or their passengers. They
could not really do otherwise than flog their tired horses
to urge them on for mile upon mile along the terrible
roads, and they were only nice to their passengers for
the sake of the tips they hoped to get out of them or the
fares they were able to pocket on the side. The good days
for the coachmen had not yet arrived; it was a rough,
hard life, underpaid and overburdened by the odds
against getting the coach successfully to its destination
without a break-down or an accident. Rotten harness,
sometimes so old it should never have been used at all,
broken axles and wheels that worked loose and fell off,
were only some of the coachman's difficulties; he sat for
hours on a box without springs directly above the front
wheels, until his legs were so cramped and sore that he
could hardly move: passengers could not expect him to
be of a meek and gentle disposition.

The good days for the passengers had not yet arrived,
either. Dean Swift, who frequently travelled the Chester
road on horseback on his journeys to and from Ireland,
once tried the stage-coach instead and wrote a satirical
description of his experience on leaving London at three
o'clock in the morning:

Roused from sound sleep—thrice called—at length
  I rise,
Yawning, stretch out my arms, half-closed my eyes;
By steps and lanthorn enter the machine,
And take my place, how cordially between
Two aged matrons of excessive bulk,
To mend the matter, too, of meaner folk;
While in like mood, jammed in on t'other side,
A bullying Captain and a fair one ride,
Foolish and fair, and in whose lap a boy—
Our plague eternal, but *her* only joy.
At last, the glorious number to complete,
Steps in my landlord for that bodkin seat;
When soon, by every hillock, rut, and stone,
In each other's faces by turn we're thrown.
This grandam scolds, *that* coughs, the Captain
  swears,
The fair one screams, and has a thousand fears;
While our plump landlord, trained in other lore,
Slumbers at ease, nor yet ashamed to snore;
And Master Dicky, in his mother's lap,
Squalling, at once brings up three meals of pap.
Sweet company! Next time, I do protest, Sir,
I'd walk to Dublin, ere I ride to Chester!

Swift did not apparently ever venture on a public coach again. Yet to the generation growing up under Queen Anne and reaching maturity in the time of King George I, there were signs of better things to come, and going by coach was considered a sufficiently refined means of travelling for Sir Richard Steele to make it the subject of an essay on morals and manners in the *Spectator*. He described how he arrived at the country town at twilight to be ready for the coach the next morning and how his servant inquired of the innkeeper what company he would have travelling with him. There were two

ladies: Mistress Betty Arable, the great fortune, and the
widow, her mother; young Squire Quickset, her cousin,
that her mother wished her to marry; Ephraim, a Quaker
who was Mistress Arable's guardian, and a recruiting
officer.

At dawn the next morning, Steele got dressed quickly,
not to keep anyone waiting or to cause any kind of dis-
pute, but the recruiting officer began to assert himself at
once by shouting at his drummer-boy to look sharp and
to place his things carefully so that none of them should
get spoilt. Finally, when the Captain's half-pike had
been put next to the coachman and his drum and his
cloak-bag behind the coach, they set off. 'We sat with
that dislike which people not too good-natured usually
conceive of each other at first sight,' Steele wrote—but
the coach jumbled them into some sort of familiarity and
they had not gone more than two miles when the widow
asked the Captain what success he had had in his recruiting. The Captain's reply was surprising; he promptly
vowed that having had no luck at all, he would be glad 'to
end his warfare in the service of her or her fair daughter',
following this up with an even more saucy proposal: 'I
am a soldier,' he said, 'and to be plain is my character:
You see me, madam, young, sound and impudent; take
me yourself, widow, or give me to her, I will be wholly at
your disposal. I am a soldier of fortune, ha!'

The ladies were reduced to silence by the Captain's
statement, whereupon, quite undaunted, he went on to
suggest that he and the young heiress should be married
at the next town and that the Quaker, whom he called 'a
smokey old fellow', should give the bride away. This was
altogether too much for Ephraim, who rebuked him
soundly. 'Friend, thy mirth savoureth of folly,' he said.
'Thou art a person of a light mind; thy drum is a type of
thee, it soundeth because it is empty. Verily it is not from
thy fullness, but from thy emptiness that thou hast

spoken.' And he then went on to deliver a lengthy homily
on the good manners necessary to travellers in a public
vehicle: 'We have hired this coach in partnership with
thee, to carry us to the great city; we cannot go any other
way. This worthy mother must hear thee, if thou wilt
needs utter thy follies; but if thou wert a man of understanding thou wouldst not take advantage of thy
courageous countenence to abash us children of peace.
Thou art, thou sayest, a soldier; give quarter to us who
cannot resist thee. If thou speakest improper things in
the hearing of this virtuous virgin, consider it as an out-
rage against a distressed person that cannot get from
thee. To speak indiscreetly what we are obliged to hear
by being hasped up in this public vehicle, is in some
degree assaulting on the high road.'

Steele, meanwhile, by pretending to be asleep, had
fallen back on the traveller's only defence against over-
talkative and boring companions. Squire Quickset also,
took no part in protecting his intended from the loose
talk of the military. But under the weight of the Quaker's
rebuke, the Captain climbed down immediately and
made a handsome apology to the ladies, promising to be
very orderly for the rest of the journey. Perhaps the
ladies themselves were a little disappointed in being done
out of their fun and did not quite agree with Steele's
rather smug conclusion that it was 'no small good-fortune
when I considered the company we were in, that the
whole journey was not spent in impertinences'; if they
did not travel very often or meet with very many good-
looking military gentlemen, they might well have found
the Captain's gallantry and his gaiety more of an
entertainment than a nuisance.

Refinement, however, and the good manners extolled
by the essayists of the Augustan Age, were beginning to
be adopted by all kinds of people, who now thought the
lewd, rumbustious behaviour of the age preceeding their

own, unseemly and a sign of ill-breeding. Two other
gentlewomen, travelling with their maid-servant on the
coach to Bath, were a model of politeness to all concerned. They insisted on paying their own bills when the
coach stopped for breakfast at Colnbrook and at Reading
for dinner, though they helped to drain the bottle of
'Right Nants' belonging to a Bristol merchant who was
travelling with them, and after this feat, one of them
told a story. At Theale, on top of the merchant's brandy,
they tasted Old Mother Cleanly's bottled ale and plum
cake at the Crown and not surprisingly, one of them fell
asleep afterwards, while the merchant was telling them
his story. At Newbury, where they spent the night, the
landlord overcharged them: 'For a brace of Midling
Trouts, a Leash of Crowns; Six shillings for a Shoulder
of Mutton and a Plate of Gerkins; Three and Sixpence
for Six Rowles, and three Nipperkins of Belch, and Two
Shillings more for Whip in drinking their health'. The
wine was good, but so was the price, and the next
morning, the angry ladies took the law into their own
hands in defiance of the landlord and prepared a pot of
chocolate of their own making.

The merchant's bottle was refilled with brandy and
they set off again for Marlborough, but the road was so
bad, the bottle got broken and this disaster spoilt their
journey to the White Hart and diminished their appetite
for breakfast. Then, as they went on, the road became
still worse—it took them three hours to cover a distance
of two miles; and when at last they reached Calne, they
found the yard of the King's Arms already crowded with
coaches and the parlour of the inn full of visitors, all
enjoying the landlady's 'Loynes of Mutton'. After Calne,
the road was again 'so Rocky, Unlevel and Narrow in
some places', the passengers thought it would have been
easier and less dangerous to have crossed the Alps with
Hannibal and his elephants, but finally they reached

Bath in the evening and the two ladies said good-bye to the Bristol merchant and went to their lodgings.

Bath had changed greatly in the fifty or sixty odd years since the first coach from London had arrived at the White Lion. Refinement and good manners were *de rigueur* since Beau Nash had become the Master of Ceremonies. His rules were strict—no boots or swords for the gentlemen, no aprons for the ladies; and no one dared to defy this extraordinary man with the brandy-coloured face crowned by a brown wig and a large, three-cornered white hat. Ever vigilant, his rather prominent watery blue eyes were to be seen at all the Balls and the Assemblies, in the Pump Room and the Gaming Rooms, quizzing the company without fear or favour. Duchesses quailed beneath his stare and rude country squires and their dames behaved with the utmost decorum as they mingled with the persons of high rank and fashion.

Building was going on everywhere in the glorious honey-coloured local stone, transforming the original narrow streets of the city, encircled by its green hills, into elegant thoroughfares, squares and crescents of houses to accommodate the vast numbers of visitors arriving daily. Everyone went there: Dr Arbuthnot, Addison, Steele, Congreve, Pope and his lady friends, the Misses Teresa and Martha Blount; the now ageing and widowed Duchess of Marlborough, the Duchess of Queensbury, Lady Mary Wortley Montagu, the Duchess of Shrewsbury and Lady Orkney;—and those who were not anybody, hoped by aping the *beau monde* to be taken for somebody.

They all had to get there somehow—by private carriage, post-chaise or the public coach; and the traffic on the road multiplied exceedingly. Beau Nash bullied the Bath Corporation into paving some of the streets in the city and insisted on the enforcement of a new

bye-law whereby householders were required to hang out
'lanthorns between the 14th September and March the
25th, as it shall grow dark until 12 o'clock at night
upon pain of forfeiting two shillings for default'. He also
set up an elaborate system of pumps on the London
road with the idea of spraying it with water to lay the
dust, yet even he, with all his authority, could do nothing
to improve the surface. The wealthy merchants of
Bristol, only twelve miles away, might have done something, if they had not been so jealous of their own independence as the second largest port in the kingdom; but
with a rich foreign trade carried by their own ships
across the seven seas, they were not interested in being
linked by faster transport on a better road through Bath
to the metropolis—they feared it, anxious to keep their
mercantile power to themselves and proud of their
dominating position in the south and south-west of
England and Wales.

Defoe, being a Londoner, was extremely critical of
the obstinate civic pride he found in the provincial cities
he visited. Yet each maintained its own distinctive
character by virtue of the distances that separated one
from the other. In 1706 it still took four days to reach
York from London, but travellers were rewarded by the
splendid sight of the Minster and the modern buildings
that were rapidly taking the place of the old fortifica-
tions, besides being able to enjoy the strongest ale in
England, Yorkshire pudding and York ham. They found,
too, a city that had become an important centre of the
coaching business. From the Black Swan in Coney Street,
they could get a coach to Newcastle, performed (if God
permit) by Benjamin Kingman, Henry Harrison and
Walter Baynes, the proprietors of the London coach;
or, if they had business in Hull or Leeds or Wakefield,
they could make their way there in one of the several
coaches scheduled to accomplish the journey.

Wakefield was a clean, large, well-built town, very populous and very rich on the clothing trade of the West Riding, with a stately stone bridge across the River Calder and the remains of a medieval castle. Leeds had a cloth market which was famous throughout the world, the clothiers setting up their stalls all along the broad main street between the first ring of the market bell at seven o'clock in the morning and the second ring an hour and a half later, by which time their bales of cloth were all sold to foreign merchants from Hamburg and the Hague, or from cities as far away as Danzig and St Petersburg. Hull likewise thrived on the cloth trade, shipping all the goods from Leeds and Wakefield over the water to their destination and receiving in return 'Muscovy linnen and yarn', oil, fruit, flax, copper and hemp from Holland and the Baltic. The go-ahead merchants of Yorkshire, the foreign buyers and traders and those who came down from London had urgent need of a good coaching service.

In some instances they were better off on the open road than in the towns, where the uneven cobbles paving the streets caused coach passengers the utmost misery. Ned Ward, a good-humoured wit, who kept a tavern near Gray's Inn and wrote *The London Spy*, which appeared regularly in monthly parts, described his experiences on reaching London: 'Our Stratford tub outran the smoothness of the road and entered upon London stones with as much frightful rumbling as an empty hay-cart, our leather conveniency having no more sway than a funeral hearse or a country waggon, so that we were jumbled about like so many peas in a child's rattle, running a great hazard of dislocation at every jolt. This we endured till we were brought within Whitechapel Bars, where we lighted from our stubborn caravan, with our elbows and shoulders as black and blue as a rural Joan that has been under the pinches of an angry fairy.'

Ward's exaggerations, though made with one eye on the entertainment of his readers, had some substance in fact: London stones were a torment. 'For my part,' he went on, 'if this be the pleasure of riding in a coach through London streets, may those who like it enjoy it, for it has loosened my joints in so short a passage, that I shall scarce recover my former strength this fortnight. I would rather choose to cry mouse-traps for a livelihood than be obliged every day to be dragged about town under such circumstances, and if the coaches of the quality are as troublesome as this, I would not be bound to do their penance for their estates.' His friend told him he had not 'the right knack of humouring the coach's motion', for there was 'as much art in sitting in a coach finely' as in riding a horse or carving up a fowl, but Ward was not convinced and to get to the other end of the town, he hobbled down to the waterside and finished his journey in a Thames wherry. He was still old-fashioned enough to prefer going by water to going by road.

5

OUTSIDERS

THE NOT SO affluent merchants, traders, shopkeepers and farmers who travelled in the rear basket, had even more need than Ned Ward of learning 'the right knack of humouring the coach's motion'. One moment they were lurching sideways, the next thrown into the air like a Jack-in-the-box and then hard down on the boxes and bundles of luggage belonging to the inside passengers; and even when coaches were improved and hung on proper springs, the 'rumble-tumble' did not benefit from them.

Nevertheless, it was the gradual improvement in coach design combined with the improved methods of road repairing in the Georgian era that brought about the alternative to riding in the basket for those who could not afford the full fare. Probably it was some drunken sailor out for a lark, who first hitched himself on to the roof of a coach, and some sharp-witted coach proprietor who saw the possibilities of turning the sailor's adventure into a profit. If the coaches carrying six inside passengers could be made to carry six or seven outside, a big saving would obviously be made in running costs. Three outsides could sit on the front part of the roof with their feet on the back of the driving-box and one on the box seat by the coachman; three more, at a pinch, could sit on the hind part of the roof, though their feet would be left dangling in the air and they would have to maintain their balance by sheer faith in their own chances of survival. They were not, after all, paying very much. If the rain poured down their necks and the wind sent their hats skimming away over the country, or the merciless sun in midsummer roasted their heads while the dust rose up to choke them, that was not the fault of the coach proprietor: outsiders simply had to be tough and in love with danger not to succumb to their ferocious ordeal.

In a picture painted by Hogarth in 1747 of a coach loading up in the yard of a country inn, an old woman, contentedly puffing at a clay pipe, can be seen already ensconced in the rear basket with a mountain of luggage hanging all round her. The coach is an old-fashioned one, shaped like an outsize funeral urn, with no windows and a step-ladder for the inside passengers to enter by. A very stout party is being pushed inside from the rear, while a bad-tempered looking gentleman argues with the land-lord about his bill and the landlady is madly ringing a bell to assemble the rest of the passengers. The couple embracing in the doorway are surely going to be late. A bored and cynical-looking captain is already sitting nonchalantly on the roof with his sword across his knees, waiting for the coach to move off, and sprawling beside him is a sinister looking yokel with his belongings tied up in a bundle. They have apparently nothing to hang on to and do not seem to be in the least concerned about their perilous position.

Not until 1753 were 'bows' or handles first provided for the outsiders to cling on to—on Fowler's London to Shrewsbury stage-coach, which in the summer of that year, advertised inside fares at one guinea and outsides at half-price, no small saving for those who were hard up and willing to test their endurance on a journey of 152 miles. The road varied, part of the way following the old Roman Watling Street where a hard surface could be maintained without too much difficulty, other sections bogged down by the clays of the Midlands, which caused the road surveyors so much trouble and the outside passengers to hang on for dear life to their bows. If they maintained their balance successfully, a fine bridge across the River Severn brought the coach clattering up a steep hill into Shrewsbury, where at last, stiff and exhausted by the strain of travelling for three and a half days, they could clamber down from their awkward perch.

Shrewsbury—until 1689 the seat of government of the Marches of Wales—still had a metropolitan character and much to offer the travellers who came there. With its sturdy, blood-red sandstone walls and the castle superbly sited above the loop of the river, its half-timbered Council House and spacious market-place, it was not only a very striking old town, patronized by all the rich and aristocratic families of Shropshire, Herefordshire and North Wales, but also a great trading centre for the agricultural products of the surrounding districts, on market day crowded with Welsh farmers, traders and small shopkeepers, drovers, pedlars and housewives, all bargaining with each other with a shrewd eye to business.

This important trading activity accounted for some of the earlier attempts made to provide cheaper travel between Shrewsbury and London, one of the most successful being achieved in 1737 by a woman. Mrs Warner was a widow of some means, the owner of a string of packhorses and of the Pheasant, a flourishing inn on Wyle Cop, the steep hill leading from the English Bridge into the town. When a soldier by the name of Carter was billetted on her, she found him so much to her liking that she presently took him for better or for worse as her second husband, whereupon he wisely gave up the brutal life of the army and settled down to help her run her business. Together they established a superior kind of stage-waggon, called the 'Gee-ho', which went to London

in seven, eight or nine days, according to the weather
and the waggoner's inclination. It was drawn by eight
horses in single file, with two more in reserve to pull it
out of the infernal mud that might be encountered anywhere along the road, and although ostensibly a vehicle
for the carriage of goods, quite a few people found it not
unpleasant and very cheap to travel lying down among
the bales of Welsh flannel and the big round cheeses that
the 'Gee-ho' transported to London.

Waggon travelling was one of the earliest known ways
of getting about the country, though not, of course, for
any traveller who considered himself a gentleman. The
distinguished Frenchman, Samuel de Sorbière, Historio-
grapher Royal to King Louis XIV made a great mistake
in 1663 when he elected to travel from Dover to London
in a waggon. He found the waggoner—'Cloathed in
Black and appointed in all things like another St George,
with a Brave Mounteero on his Head—a Merry Fellow,
who fancy'd he made a Figure and seemed mighty
pleased with himself.' But none of the innkeepers where
the waggon stopped 'took Care as they ought of a
Stranger, who could not tell how to make the People
understand him'—in fact, he complained: 'I was as little
regarded as if I had been a bale of goods'; and as he had
already been chased in the streets of Dover by a horde of
abusive children, it was not surprising that de Sorbière's
first impressions of England was a very poor one.

The stage-waggons, with their big canvas tilts and
roomy interior, were, none the less, a very good friend to
the poor. Anyone could walk faster than the waggons
moved, but speed in the early years of the eighteenth
century was neither a mania nor a god, and it was much
more cosy to travel in company than to go alone. The
waggoners, who walked or rode beside their horses and
urged them on with an abracadabra of horsey language
that no one else could understand, were, on the whole,

good-natured individuals whose experience of all kinds
of weather and all kinds of men encouraged them to be
philosophical. They settled disputes between their
passengers, did countless errands for the villagers, the
barmaids and the innkeepers down the road and on May
Day, when spring had returned to the hills and the fields,
they decked their horses and themselves with coloured
ribbons. The tinkling bells on the horses' harness and the
merry songs the waggoners sang as they trudged along,
were a welcome sound in the deep silence of the country
and it was not for nothing that several inns were named
after them, the Jolly Waggoner becoming a sign as
popular as the Jolly Sailor or the Coach and Horses.

Smollett in describing the adventures of Roderick
Random on his journey up to London, showed much
more respect for Joey, the waggoner, than for any of his
passengers and these were, indeed, a rag-bag of human
folly: the sham Captain Weazel, really a valet in disguise,
whose 'Blood and wounds! Hell and damnation!' were
the empty brag of a craven heart quite white with fear
and apprehension; his kept woman, who gave herself the
airs of a great lady and 'wished to God they had writ for
the chariot' to take them on their journey; Miss Jenny, a
wanton baggage, wearing a silver laced hat on her head
instead of a cap and a blue stuff riding-suit trimmed with
silver lace, 'very much tarnished', who was about to
resume her former way of life after a disastrous affair
with a recruiting officer; and the old rogue who was
chasing her, one Isaac, a Jewish money-lender, with a
face 'shrivelled into a thousand wrinkles, a nose so sharp
and drooping and a chin so peaked and prominent, that
when he mumped or spoke, they approached one another
like a pair of nutcrackers'.

This ill-assorted quartet and Roderick's friend, Strap,
got up to all sorts of indecent pranks when they spent the
night at one of the inns on the road and thus were made

to serve Smollett's purpose in writing a picaresque
humorous novel of the times. Yet Smollett, like Defoe,
used his own observation as well as his imagination, and
his characters truly belonged to the lusty, brawling
world of the common people that he knew from experience. Their unhappy adventure when they arrived at one
of the inns to find their dinner had been commandeered
by three gentlemen travelling in a private carriage, was
one that actually happened to travellers on the waggon.
The gentlemen thought it would do the waggon people no
harm 'to dine upon bread and cheese for one day', adding
that 'their betters must be served before them', and this
was the general attitude of the gentry to the common
people throughout the whole of the Georgian era. Lords
and ladies, travelling in private, looked down on the
stage-coach passengers; inside passengers on the coach
looked down on the outsiders, refusing to sit with them
at dinner, while everyone looked with the utmost
contempt on the poor folk travelling in the waggons, who
had no one left to look down upon, except the wayfarers
on foot.

Yet the man whose bulky image came to dominate so
much of the eighteenth century, the poor scholar in a
snuff-coloured coat and a wig 'that often wanted powder',
could not afford the coach or the waggon when he first
travelled from Lichfield to London in 1737. Samuel
Johnson 'rode and tied' with his young friend, David
Garrick; they had one horse between them which they
rode in turns and tethered until the one on foot caught up.
Garrick had three half-pence in his pocket when they
arrived in London, Johnson exactly twopence half-penny
—and he never forgot it. The actor, when he had become
rich and successful, looked back on their journey with a
laugh; Johnson never saw it as a joke. To him it was a
constant reminder of the gulf between the rich and the
poor, and for all his enjoyment in later life of the afflu-

ence surrounding his friends, the Thrales, and their
entertainment of him at Streatham, the Grand Cham of
letters was always biased in favour of the deserving poor.
He understood their predicament and, with all the weight
of his moral authority, came down on their side.

To some visitors from abroad, these distinctions
between rich and poor were very curious and uncomfortable. Carl Philippe Moritz, a German pastor, who
came over from Hamburg in 1782, was young and
vulnerable and far from rich. When he was tired of
walking on the road from Hounslow to Maidenhead, he
liked to sit in the shade of a hedge and read Milton. 'But
this relief was soon rendered disagreeable to me,' he
wrote, 'for those who rode and drove past me, stared at
me with astonishment and made many significant
gestures as if they thought my mind deranged.' And even
more disagreeable was the treatment he received when
trying to find a lodging in Windsor. At the first inn he was
shown a room which 'much resembled a prison for
malefactors' and when he asked for a better one, was
rudely told to go on to Slough, whereupon he tried to
console himself with the thought that this 'impudent
ill-usage' from people who were but servants of the public
was not likely to reflect well on themselves or to recom-
mend them to their betters.

Eventually Moritz found a civil innkeeper, who gave
him a room that he had to share with a drunken man who
went to bed in his boots. He did not mind this quite so
much as he minded the off-hand way in which the innkeeper's staff treated him. 'As I entered and desired to
have something to eat, the countenance of the waiter
soon gave me to understand that I should there find no
friendly reception,' he commented. 'Whatever I got they
seemed to give me with such an air as showed too
plainly how little they thought of me, and as if they
considered me but as a beggar. I must do them justice to

own however that they suffered me to pay like a gentleman. No doubt this was the first time that this pert,
bepowdered puppy had ever been called upon to wait on
a poor devil who entered their place on foot.'

The pastor certainly paid like a gentleman and was
thoroughly fleeced. His accommodation with the drunken
man in boots and his supper off a tough old fowl cost him
9s., and the 'pert, bepowdered puppy' and the chambermaid both demanded a tip as he was leaving, which was
more than his thrifty German nature could tolerate. He
gave the waiter three half-pence and was promptly
saluted with 'the heartiest God damn you, Sir' that he
had ever heard, which perhaps gave him the courage to
tell the chambermaid that he could not reward her
'shameful incivility' with anything.

At Oxford, though again arriving on foot, he was more
fortunate: a friend introduced him to the landlord at the
Mitre, where he found 'prince-like attendance' and was
very content. But his adventures in travelling by coach
were far less happy, for without in the least knowing
what he would have to endure, he chose to go from
Leicester to Northampton as an outsider. 'This ride I
shall remember as long as I live,' he wrote. 'The inside
passengers got into the coach from the yard, but we on
the outside were obliged to clamber up in the street,
because we should have had no room for our heads to
pass under the gateway. My companions on top of the
coach were a farmer, a young man very decently dressed
and a blackamoor. The getting up alone was at the risk
of one's life, and when I was up I was obliged to sit just
at the corner of the coach, with nothing to hold on by
but a sort of little handle fastened on the side. I sat
nearest the wheel, and the moment that we set off I
fancied I saw certain death before me. All I could do was
to take still faster hold of the handle and to be more
careful to preserve my balance. The machine now rolled

along with prodigious rapidity over the stones through the town of Leicester, and every moment seemed to fly in the air; so that it was almost a miracle that we still stuck to the coach and did not fall. . . . '

Poor Moritz!—he was in need of all the faith he could muster; his troubles had only just begun. 'At last,' he went on, 'the being continually in fear of my life became insupportable, and as we were going up a hill and consequently proceeding rather slower than usual, I crept from the top of the coach and got myself snugly ensconced in the basket behind. "Oh, Sir, you will be shaken to death!" said the blackamoor, but I heeded him not, trusting that he was exaggerating the unpleasantness of my new situation. And, truly, as long as we went on slowly up the hill, it was easy and pleasant enough, and I was just on the point of falling asleep, when on a sudden the coach proceeded at a rapid rate downhill. Then all the boxes, iron-nailed and copper-fastened, began to dance round me; everything in the basket appeared to be alive and every moment I received such violent blows that I thought my last hour was come. The blackamoor had been right, but repentance was useless, and I was obliged to suffer horrible torture for nearly an hour, which seemed to me an eternity . . . until at last we came to another hill, when quite shaken to pieces, bleeding and sore, I ruefully crept back to the top of the the coach and took possession of my former seat.'

Here the unfortunate pastor remained for the rest of his journey, but it rained incessantly from Harborough to Northampton and the decently dressed young man kept on falling asleep and rolling against him, nearly pushing him from his seat, to which he clung 'with the last strength of despair', cold and wet and utterly miserable. 'My forces were nearly giving way, when at last, happily, we reached Northampton,' he concluded, 'and I now write this as a warning to all strangers who

are inclined to ride in English stage-coaches and take an
outside seat, or, worse still, horror of horrors, a seat in
the basket.'

Moritz looked carefully into his purse after this
terrifying experience and took an inside place on the
coach from Northampton to London, before leaving for
Hamburg. His anxious warning, whether or not it was
heeded by any of his countrymen who came to England,
made no appeal to the English themselves. They continued to ride outside or in the basket and to find it a
cheap and convenient way of getting about. But there
was, of course, nothing new in foreigners believing that
all the English were a little mad—and there was nothing
new, either, in the belief of the English in their own
superiority.

6

FASTER
TRAVEL

ENGLISHMEN OF THE eighteenth century had some cause to be proud of themselves and of the age they were living in. Personal freedom was more secure than in any previous generation and more highly prized in England than anywhere abroad. Wealth and leisure were on the increase and more widely diffused than ever before. Not only the aristocratic families, but 'the middling sort' as they were called then, the merchants, traders, farmers, innkeepers, shopkeepers and craftsmen were enjoying an era of peace and plenty such as England had never known. As yet there was no great development of factories producing goods wholesale; individual crafts-men, weavers, stocking-makers, blacksmiths, carpenters and candle-makers still worked in their own homes or in small units in the towns, and they were never far from the land which had bred them and nursed them up. Enough food was grown to feed the whole population and though the poor in the underworld of the towns and cities lived like the rats infesting the sewers, in the country they were cared for by the parish and other charitable funds. Their 'betters' might insist on being properly respected, yet they were not unmindful of their

duty to those less fortunate than themselves and there
was very little ill-feeling or warfare between the classes.
The squire, who was often also Justice of the Peace,
could be at his best a benevolent father to his people,
and village life was still the backbone of the nation.

It was, however, the expansion of trade and the
growing importance of the towns that called for better
communications throughout the country, and between
1730 and 1780 some sixteen hundred Road Acts were
passed through Parliament extending the turnpike
system to many more of the major highways in the
kingdom. Coach proprietors, though they grumbled at
having to pay so many tolls, were quick to take advantage of the better roads; coach-builders were able to
think out new methods of designing more comfortable
vehicles. Thus from about 1730 onwards, more and more
advertisements appeared for 'Flying Machines' and
'Glass Coaches', and more and more people began to
travel long distances, thereby changing their outlook on
life more profoundly than they at first realized.

Much of the new coaching business was initiated in
the Midlands and the North, the provincial towns being
more anxious to link themselves with London than
London, with its near monopoly of trade, was to be
linked with them. In 1731 Nicholas Rothwell of Warwick
was the first and only coach-master, or 'undertaker', to
run a stage between Birmingham and London. It went
through Warwick, Banbury and Aylesbury and took
two and a half days, the passengers paying 21s. for the
whole journey and 18s. from Warwick to London.
Rothwell on the same bill advertised his willingness 'to
furnish all persons with a By-coach, Chariot, Chaise or
Hearse, with a mourning Coach and able Horses to any
Part of Great Britain, at reasonable Rates'—a fair
enough offer to the living and the dead and one that
showed the extensiveness of his business. Ten years later

there was a 'Flying Coach' between Birmingham and London, and by 1748 an 'Improved Birmingham Coach', which boldly announced that 'friction was annihilated', the axles being fitted with a wonderful new device, which proved to be rather unreliable but was intended to comfort the living even if it was of no consequence to the dead.

In 1751 an advertisement for the new 'Expedition Coach' from Norwich to London announced that it would leave the Maid's Head on Wednesday or Thursday morning at seven o'clock and arrive at the Boar in Aldgate on Friday or Saturday 'as shall seem good' to the passengers who favoured it with their custom and were not in a great hurry to reach their destination. This, however, was not good enough for the enterprising businessmen living farther north or in the Midlands. Manchester, not to be outdone by Birmingham, started a direct service to London in 1754, declaring that 'however incredible it may appear, this coach will actually (barring accidents) arrive in London in four days and a half after leaving Manchester'. Liverpool with a 'Flying Machine' and Leeds with a 'Flying Coach' followed the lead of Birmingham and Manchester, but when the Liverpool coach covered the journey of 206 miles in three days, some people began to think that travelling was becoming altogether too hectic. Innkeepers believed that their business of lodging travellers for the night would suffer a decline. They talked nostalgically of the good old days when coaches might be held up for three or four days by the weather and travelling was sufficiently slow to allow the passengers two hours for their dinner and then some time over, if the coachman was polite enough to suggest that he did not want to disturb them 'if they wished for another bottle'.

Only the more far-sighted among the innkeepers realized that faster travel meant more coaches on the

road and an ever-increasing number of travellers. But
Arthur Young, a journalist, who toured England in the
seventeen-sixties and had the interests of the country
very much at heart, saw another and more serious
danger. 'To find fault with good roads would have the
appearance of paradox and absurdity,' he wrote, 'but it
is nevertheless a fact that giving the power of expeditious travelling depopulates the kingdom. Young men
and women in the country villages fix their eyes on
London as the last stage of their hope. They enter into
service in the country for little else but to raise money
enough to go to London, which was no such easy matter
when a stage-coach was four or five days in creeping a
hundred miles. The fare and the expenses ran high. *But
now*! a country fellow, one hundred miles from London,
jumps on a coach box in the morning and for eight or ten
shillings gets to town by night, which makes a material
difference; besides rendering the going up and down so
easy, the numbers *who have seen London* are increased
tenfold, and of course ten times the boasts are sounded
in the ears of the country fools to induce them to quit
their healthy clean fields for a region of dirt, stink and
noise.' Here indeed was the beginning of the exodus from
the country to the town which was to gather momentum
as time went on, and Arthur Young was among the
first to realize that there was no way of stopping it.
Change was in the air and England could not travel
backwards. Her coaches were gathering speed towards
the unforeseeable future and many more people were
travelling on them.

Most of the passengers came from the middling sort
and their reticent behaviour at the beginning of a
journey was noticed by Count Kielmansegge, another
German visitor, who came to England some twenty
years earlier than Pastor Moritz. 'The first sight of
people of different classes and sexes, who are perfectly

unknown to each other, occasions a deep silence,' the Count wrote, 'as nobody knows what to make of his neighbour or how to begin a conversation. At last some-one begins to talk of the road and the weather; this gradually brings up other subjects, such as how long one is on the road etc. A political discussion is sure to follow, especially with English people, so that gradually you get better acquainted and time passes until you arrive at your destination, where on alighting, you find dinner ready for you.'

But the Count, who had come to England with his brother to attend the Coronation of King George III, considered it was rather beneath his dignity to travel by the public coach at all and he would not have done so if Prince Charles of Mecklenburg, preceding him on his way to attend a naval review at Portsmouth, had not commandeered all the horses from the posting-inn at Godalming. The Count's only consolation was that the same fate had befallen a certain Captain Campbell, who, with his young and handsome wife, had been waiting since one o'clock at Godalming for want of horses and so was also forced to take the coach as a makeshift. The young couple had been married only four months before in Edinburgh and were about to join a ship sailing for the East Indies, and when Count Kielmansegge dis-covered that the bride was related to the Duke of Argyll, she went up in his estimation, so that he managed to pass the time without being bored by her company and to put up with the two other young men and the skipper's wife, who shared the coach with them.

'Meanwhile an adventure was not wanting,' the Count wrote afterwards in his journal, 'as there was a quarrel between our coachman and a cart-driver, who had to make room for us. This occasioned a fight which was settled by three of the men passengers in the coach and my servant, who was sitting behind, coming to the aid of

the coachman and making the carter get out of the way
by using force and administering a good licking, thus
gaining victory; whilst I, as a careful strategist, guarded
the baggage and the coach with the lady inside and
formed the *corps de reserve* so as to cover the retreat in
case of necessity.'

The Count finally reached Portsmouth at seven o'clock
in the evening, none the worse for his journey. But his
brother, who could not get a seat in the same coach, was
less fortunate. He travelled all the way in the company of
a fat, English innkeeper's wife, who kept her brandy
bottle handy, two sailors' wives and one other man, who
was the only one of the party with whom he could con-
verse and who left the coach after the first four miles,
abandoning the noble Hanoverian to his silent and stern
disapproval of the bibulous and corpulent innkeeper's
lady.

Lack of conversation between passengers who disliked
the look of each other, or the difficulties of beginning a
conversation among strangers, had already been observed
by Dr Johnson in the description of a stage-coach journey
which he wrote for the *Adventurer* in 1754. No longer
obliged to ride and tie as he had from Lichfield in 1737,
he found the pretentious air of gentility among his fellow
passengers regrettable. 'It was easy to observe the affected elevation of mien with which everyone entered the
coach, and the supercilious civility with which they paid
compliments to each other,' he wrote. 'When the first
ceremony was dispatched we sat silent for a long time,
all employed in collecting importance into our faces and
endeavouring to strike reverence and submission into
our companions. . . . At last a corpulent gentleman, who
had equipped himself for this expedition with a scarlet
surtout and a large hat with a broad lace, drew out his
watch, looked on it in silence, and then held it dangling
at his finger. This was, I suppose, understood by all the

company as an invitation to ask the time of day, but nobody appeared to heed his overture; and his desire to be
talking so far overcame his resentment, that he let us
know of his own accord that it was past five and that in
two hours we should be at breakfast.'

This opening gambit did not appeal to any of the other
travellers or make them more friendly: the two ladies
held up their heads in silence, one of the young men
stared out of the window as if absorbed in counting the
trees, the other closed his eyes, pretending to be asleep,
while Johnson amused himself by watching their behaviour. Breakfast, however, was quite a different
matter; it suddenly loosened their tongues. The gentleman in the scarlet surtout began to talk about his
acquaintance with Lord Mumble and the Duke of Ten-
terden, and one of the ladies, when compelled to reach
across the table for a dish of ham, remarked on the
inconveniencies of travelling and 'the difficulty which
they who never sat at home without a great number of
attendants found in performing for themselves such
offices as the road required', further suggesting that she
numbered herself among the persons of quality who
often travelled *incognito*. One of the young men then
called for a newspaper and after studying it for some
time began to boast about buying and selling stocks to
the tune of £30,000 on the London Exchange, while the
other young man, who said he was intimate with the
Lord Chancellor and judges of the High Court, capped
this by asserting that in his opinion the only sure way of
investing money was in real estate.

'It might be expected that upon these glimpses of
latent dignity, we should all have begun to look round
us with veneration,' Johnson continued. 'Yet it happened
that none of these hints made much impression on the
company; everyone was apparently suspected of endeavouring to impose false appearances on the rest; all

continued their haughtiness, in hopes to enforce their
claims; and all grew every hour more sullen, because they
found their representation of themselves without effect.
. . . Thus we travelled on, four days, with malevolence
perpetually increasing, and without any endeavour but
to outvie each other in superciliousness and neglect; and
when any two of us could separate for a moment, we
vented our indignation at the sauciness of the rest.'

Only when the long journey came to an end was the
true identity of the passengers revealed. The stout
gentleman in the surtout, boasting of his intimacy with
lords and dukes, was a nobleman's butler, who had furnished a shop with the money he had saved. The young
man who had talked of risking £30,000 in the funds, was
a clerk to a broker in 'Change-Alley', and the other
young man who had friends among the High Court
judges, a lawyer's clerk living in a garret in the Temple.
The lady, who so carefully concealed her quality, kept
a cook-shop behind the Exchange and probably served
her customers with more than a dish of ham; the other
lady was the only one among them who had 'assumed no
character, but accomodated herself to the scene before
her without any struggle for distinction or superiority'.

Johnson reflected sadly on the folly of such people—
and there were many in his time—whose false pretences
designed to deceive everyone else, could only end in a
form of self-deception that would finally destroy whatever original virtue they happened to possess. With such
companions his journey could not have been a happy
one; yet he often found the public coach a convenient
way of travelling and in 1784, when he was old and ill
with dropsy and asthma, he made his last journey to
Lichfield in a stage-coach. Afterwards he wrote cour-
ageously to tell Dr Brocklesby that although he could
not have borne such violent agitation for many days
together, the first day was performed with very little

sense of fatigue and the second brought him to Lichfield
'without much lassitude'. In the coach he read the
Ciceronianus of Erasmus and, his mind being thus occupied, attempted to ignore the pain that the cruel jolting
of the vehicle gave to his swollen body.

Earlier in his life, he had always enjoyed travelling by
post-chaise and it was by this means that he journeyed
to Newcastle in 1773 before going on to Edinburgh to
meet Boswell. The post-chaise, a lighter vehicle than the
stage-coach, could be hired to carry one or two passengers and their luggage from one point to another along
the road. Painted yellow with two or four horses, one of
them ridden by a post-boy in a yellow jacket, they were
more genteel and faster, though much more expensive
than the stage-coach, and they had the added disadvan-
tage of the passengers having to change themselves and
their luggage over into a different post-chaise at the end
of every stage. But Johnson evidently travelled light.
He wore a full suit of plain brown clothes, with twisted
hair buttons of the same colour, a large bushy greyish
wig, a plain shirt, black worsted stockings and—his only
concession to any sort of display—shoes with silver
buckles. For bad weather he changed into boots and put
on a very wide brown cloth great coat, with pockets so
enormous they might have held the two volumes of his
folio *Dictionary* and were never not stuffed with books
and papers. Some clean linen, a large English oak stick
and a very old leather purse sufficed for the rest of his
needs. The purse was important: a journey by post-
chaise from London to Newcastle and on to Edinburgh
could cost anything up to £70 or £80 and Johnson was
lucky in being able to share the expense with his friend,
Mr Justice Chambers, who travelled with him.

By post-chaise or stage-coach to Newcastle and
Edinburgh, travellers were bound to follow the Great
North Road all the way and, except that the inns on the

road were some of the best in the kingdom, it was very
tiring and a very long haul. From Islington through
Holloway, Highgate, Finchley and Barnet to Hatfield
and Stevenage; then on past fields of parsnips, cucumbers
beans and peas in the rich and fertile countryside of the
market gardeners to Baldock, Biggleswade, St Neots
and Huntingdon, fifty-nine miles from London. Here the
landlord of the George provided an excellent supper with
wine and ale and beds at 2s. 6d. Then came Alconbury, a
bleak and windy hill, where the coachmen asked the
passengers to get out and walk and the Wheatsheaf
stood by the road to refresh them. Then on to the Bell at
Stilton, already famous for its cheese, made by a Mrs
Paulet of Wymondham and brought on to the table by
the landlord of the Bell with the cheese-mites or maggots
crawling all round it ready to be scooped up in a spoon
and eaten all together, but where one lady in 1756,
Mrs Calderwood, found fault with the linen, which was all
in 'perfit rags with fifty holes in each towell', presumably
the result of the laundry-maid's rubbing and not of the
cheese-mites' appetite.

After Stilton, a short stop at Kate's Cabin just beyond
Norman Cross and on through Water Newton and
Wansford, past the long wall of Burghley Park and on
over the hump-backed bridge across the River Welland
into Stamford, an historic town in grey stone, where the
stately churches and the comfortable inns not only gave
satisfaction to the soul and the body, but were united in
1765 in the marriage of Margaret Hodgson, the daughter
of the innkeeper at the George with a clergyman, the
Rev. Beilby Porteous, who afterwards became Bishop of
Chester and Bishop of London. At the George, with its
gallows sign hung right across the road, there were two
large pannelled rooms either side of the gateway from the
yard—the York Room where passengers bound for the
north waited for the coach and the London Room where

those travelling south could take their ease, read the newspapers and imbibe whatever kind of hot liquor they fancied.

On again from Stamford, the coach passed the turn-pike gate at Horn Lane, from Lincolnshire into Rutland-shire and back again into Lincolnshire across Witham Common, a notorious stretch of the road for highway robbery, to the Black Bull at Witham Corner and down the steep and dangerous Spitalgate Hill into Grantham, one hundred and ten miles from London. Here there were several inns of outstanding quality and the Angel, going back to the thirteenth century, was said to be one of the finest in the kingdom. Here also, between supper and going to bed, travellers not too exhausted by their journey could find entertainment at the theatre, which was patronized by the local gentry and visited by Garrick himself on his summer tours.

But there was still a long way to go: through Newark, where in the bad old days of the seventeenth century the landlord of the Talbot had been in league with 'Swift Nicks', the most daring highwayman of the north; over the Trent at Muskham, then on through Tuxford and Retford to the Bell at Barnby Moor; and on to Bawtry and Doncaster, where the landlord of the Angel, who was also mayor of the town and post-master, kept a pack of hounds and at one time 'lived as great as any gentleman ordinarily did'. At Ferrybridge there was the Swan, at Wetherby another Angel and in York any number of inns to welcome the travellers, who by then could pride them-selves on having come one hundred and ninety-eight miles from London.

From York the road went on, north to the market town of Thirsk and on again to Northallerton, Darling-ton, Ferryhill and Durham, where the windows of the Red Lion commanded a delightful prospect of the river, the surrounding country and the city with its massive

cathedral for any of the travellers who were not half
dead with weariness or quite incapable of keeping their
eyes open. And now with two hundred and sixty-one
miles behind them, they had only fourteen more to go,
through Chester-le-Street, past the pits and the mountains of coal already excavated, into the smoky, bustling
Tyneside town itself, where the river was black with
coal-ships waiting to take their cargo to London.

Newcastle was two hundred and seventy-five miles
from London. In 1734 the 'Flying Coach' took nine days
to get there and travellers going on to Edinburgh had
another three days and three nights on the worst and
most difficult stretch of the Great North Road through
Morpeth, Alnwick and Belford and over the border at
Berwick-on-Tweed, on to Coldingham, Dunbar and
Haddington, before they trundled into the Scottish
capital. But by 1773 when Johnson returned by the
coach from his visit to Scotland, the time had been cut
by half. 'I came home last night, without any incom-
modity, danger or weariness,' he wrote in a letter to
Boswell, 'and am ready to begin a new journey'—and
this in the month of November, notoriously bad for mist
and fog and rain and floods, with the daylight fading in
the early evening and the long night never secure except
by the blazing fire of a roadside inn.

7

TRAVELLING
IN
SCOTLAND

THE FASTER AND more certain travel that Johnson enjoyed on his journey home from Scotland in 1773 had not been won without the greatest difficulty. Travellers in the seventeenth century when they got into the first direct coach from London to Edinburgh at '£4 apeece', did not know when, if ever, they would reach their destination and several later attempts to maintain a direct service between London and the Scottish capital had failed. One apologetic coach proprietor in 1722 put a notice in the *Caledonian Mercury*, which said: 'Whereas it hath been reported that the Stage Coach to London hath not performed in Nine Days as was promised by their Bills. Now this may Satisfie. That the Badness of the weather and the Roads beat down the Horses of a sudden, which could not be prevented by the Undertaker, but for the future 'twill be punctually performed at least until Michaelmas.'

Probably the undertaker was again being too optimistic. Apart from his difficulties with storm and tempest on the road, it is doubtful if at this time there was much public support for his venture. The Scots and the English were not on the best of terms. The feelings that ran high in the first Jacobite Rebellion of 1715, slumbered and smoked underground for thirty years before exploding again in the second and more serious rising led by Bonnie Prince Charlie in 1745. In this, the courageous figure of the Young Pretender appealed to the romantic spirit of his countrymen and the English, made complacent by years of peace and prosperity, were caught napping by the wild Highlanders with their naked swords and skirling pipes, who marched as far south as Derby. By the hasty recall of the English army that had fought at Dettingen and Fontenoy and their superior discipline, the Highlanders were driven back into the hills from whence they had come; but General Wade and his chief engineer, Captain Birt, found the roads across the Border non-existent and it was only after the English victory at Culloden, that they were able to set about constructing new highways to the garrison towns they established all over the country.

Captain Birt was justly proud of his own work. 'The roads on these moors are now as smooth as Constitution Hill, and I have gallopped on some of them for miles together in great tranquility, which was heightened by reflection of my former fatigue,' he wrote, with all the zeal of an efficient officer and perhaps some pardonable exaggeration. He was not to know that the roads he built linking Stirling, Aberfeldy, Inverness and Fort William would be allowed to fall into disrepair almost as soon as the danger of any further rising was over. No one was really responsible for maintaining them, and the miller of Crieff when he dug a clay pit in the middle of one of them, thereby causing the death of a horseman, was not breaking the law: with a fine simplicity he had only to show that he could not find any clay anywhere else to be acquitted of manslaughter.

In these circumstances it is not surprising that coaching in Scotland made slow progress and that in many parts of the country, wheeled traffic was quite unknown. Captain Birt wrote from Aberdeen of 'the Surprise and Amusement of the Common People of this Town when a chariot with six monstrous great Horses arrived here by way of the Sea Coast', further suggesting that an elephant publicly exhibited in the streets of London could not have excited greater admiration; and it was, indeed, only by sea that travellers were able to approach the far north with any certainty of arriving. The one and only stage-coach that succeeded in surviving in the early years of the eighteenth century ran on the short journey from Edinburgh to Leith and back again, taking one hour to cover the one-and-a-half-mile trip. It was a three-horse chariot, painted yellow like a post-chaise, but big enough to carry six passengers and for many years a source of wonder to those who watched its gay progress from the capital to the little seaport, where many of the ships from Newcastle or London landed their passengers.

The long journey from London was, however, given a tremendous boost in 1754, when Hosea Eastgate of Soho announced that 'the Edinburgh Stage-Coach for the better Accommodation of Passengers, will be altered to a new genteel Two-end Glass Machine, hung on Steel Springs, exceeding light and easy, to go in ten Days in Summer and twelve in Winter, to set out the first Tuesday in March and continue it from Hosea Eastgate's, the Coach and Horses in Dean Street, Soho, London, and from John Somervell's in the Canongate, Edinburgh.'

Here was a coach *de-luxe* and a novelty, if the steel springs did not come apart on the journey. But the travellers who took advantage of Hosea Eastgate's offer to carry them to the Scottish capital in his new Two-end Glass Machine (and to take care of 'small Parcels, paying according to their value') found little comfort when they arrived in Edinburgh or wanted to travel beyond it. They all complained bitterly of the inns, one writer declaring that he had never seen such mean buildings or such dirty and dismal apartments and that a stranger arriving at any one of them might well be shocked 'by the novelty of being shown in by a dirty sunburned wench, without shoes or stockings'. The eating-house and dormitory on the upper floor was scarcely distinguishable from the stables below, and even at the best of the inns in the Canongate, called Boyd's or the White Horse, the waiter picked up a lump of sugar in his

THE EDINBURGH STAGE-COACH, for the better Accommodation of Paffengers, will be altered to a new genteel Two-end Glafs Machine, hung on Steel Springs, exceeding light and eafy, to go in ten Days in Summer and twelve in Winter, to fet out the firft Tuefday in March, and continue it from Hofea Eaftgate's, the Coach and Horfes in Dean-ftreet, Soho, LONDON, and from John Somervell's in the Canon gate, Edinburgh, every other Tuefday, and meet at Burrow-bridge on Saturday Night, and fet out from thence on Monday Morning, and get to London and Edinburgh on Friday. In the Winterao fet out from London and Edinburgh every other Monday Morning, and to get to Burrow-bridge on Saturday Night; and to fet out from thence on Monday Morning, and get to London and Edinburgh on Saturday Night. - Paffengers to pay as ufual. Perform'd, if Gop permits, by your dutiful Servant,   HOSEA EASTGATE.

Care is taken of fmall Parcels, paying according to their Value.

Hosea Eastgate's advertisement for his New
Glass Machine to Edinburgh, 1754

greasy fingers and put it into Dr Johnson's lemonade, whereupon the Doctor in terrible indignation flung the entire contents out of the window. Boswell also found it necessary to apologize for 'the evening effluvia' in the streets, there being no covered sewers in the town, and he was not surprised when Johnson grumbled in his ear: 'I smell you in the dark.'

None the less, by this time the common people no longer jeered and laughed at strangers arriving at the Canongate by coach and a few of the Scots themselves were beginning to take advantage of the new form of transport. Since 1750 there had been a regular 'Caravan' between Edinburgh and Glasgow, which took two days, sleeping *en route* at Falkirk, and ten years later there was a 'Fly Coach', 'commodiously fitted to hold six, secured from all weather after the best English manner', which went every day of the week, except Sundays, travel not being considered appropriate to the Lord's Day. Drysdale's, Cameron's and Mackay's whisky-shops served as booking-offices for the coach to Glasgow and others that went to Stirling and Perth. To get there from the Canongate cost 1s. 6d. in a sedan chair, walking through the filthy, muddy streets being quite out of the question for anyone who valued the cleanliness of his attire or for ladies with long skirts and thin slippers. A good many drams were consumed at the whisky-shops before setting out—and they were needed, for the roads were still a nightmare.

Travellers to Glasgow went through Linlithgow, Falkirk and Kilsyth and had to endure such a bone-shaking experience that the celebrated actress, Mrs Bellamy, refused to take her cage of pet canaries in the coach with her and instead paid a porter ten guineas which she could ill afford, to carry them from Glasgow to Edinburgh on foot. And for all the pride that the people of Glasgow had in their own city, there was no inn of any standing until Mr Tennent of the brewing firm built the Saracen's Head in 1755.

Travellers going to Perth from Edinburgh had to cross the Forth by the ancient barge across the Queensferry narrows, the passengers going aboard in the coach and wondering whether the surly boatman would ever get them safely to the other side. After this there was a terrible zig-zag climb to the top of the gorge through Inverkeithing and another hill to Kirk o'Beath and Cant's Dam before Kinross was reached. Anything might happen. The horses might stumble or go berserk, or an axle might break in the trickiest part of the journey. Ladies who were coach-sick, or suffering from vertigo, were liable to become quite hysterical and gentlemen quite white with anxiety on their account. The roads were 'deep in mire as though unmade since the Deluge, very intricate and difficult', or covered in great boulders of rocky, stumpy stone capable of upsetting the coach altogether; and the inns were no compensation, being dank and dirty and only fit for drovers.

From Kinross the coach took to the hills by Glenfarg, toiling on through the Ochils down to Wicks o'Baiglie and up again to Craigend Brae, before the sudden and breath-taking panorama of the fair city of Perth, half-islanded in the sweep of the River Tay, at last came into view. But Perth was the very end of civilization. Beyond it the wild glens were impassable for all but the most courageous, and before the Romantic Movement in poetry and painting had awakened an interest in the beauty of mountain scenery, the barren peaks with the clouds swirling round them and the fearsome, lonely gorges were considered to be 'horrid' in more ways than one. Few travellers dared to explore them. Thomas Pennant, touring on horseback in 1769, wrote of his journey from Blair Atholl to Braemar: 'The road is the most dangerous and horrible I have ever travelled; a narrow path so rugged that our horses were often obliged to cross their legs in order to pick a secure place for their feet; while, at a considerable and precipitous depth below, roared a black torrent, rolling through a bed of rock, solid in every part but where the antient Tilt had worn its way.' Roads, in fact, were still non-existent and touring in Scotland a most perilous occupation.

Yet for the curious and the cultured Englishman there was a certain horrible kind of fascination in discovering the Highlands. Sylas Neville, who went up to Edinburgh at the age of thirty to study medicine, quite enjoyed the tour he made in 1775, though he was a very nervous young man, who suffered greatly from pains in his stomach as well as from constant financial anxiety and the embarrassing entanglement he had got himself into with his so-called housekeeper, Sally Russell. In the Highlands he managed to forget some of his troubles while observing the rugged grandeur of Killicrankie and 'the hoggish manner' in which the Highlanders lived. It poured with rain and he got soaked to the skin and the inns were so unpleasant that he could not sleep without taking opium; but when he returned to Edinburgh, he came back to his more serious troubles and in the January of the following year was terribly worried about having to send Sally away to Newcastle in a storm of frost and snow, which he thought might hold up the coach and bring on a miscarriage. She was, it seems, taken ill on the road, which must have been very distressing both for her and the other passengers, but a month later she was back in Edinburgh, having left her baby with a nurse in Newcastle, and Neville's somewhat uneasy housekeeping with her continued.

The attachment had been going on for two or three years before Sylas first went to Edinburgh—ever since he had engaged Sally as his housekeeper after meeting her in Eastbourne, where she had already had a child by a certain disreputable Major Bland. Being a mixture of puritanism, romanticism and priggishness, Sylas quite honestly believed that it was his 'benevolence' which had induced him to take her away from her native place where 'her reputation had been blasted' and to set her up elsewhere. Though he could ill afford it, he rented a house at Scratby, near Norwich, and when they were settled, sent Sally back to Eastbourne to fetch her young daughter. Afterwards he made a detailed copy in his diary of her expenses for the journey into Sussex and back:

July 1.	Coach hire to Norwich inside	3	o
	Dinner there for lad Tom and self	6	6
2.	Coach to London outside	11	o
5.	Do. from London to Lewes	6	6
	Hire of horse and man from Lewes to East Bourne	7	o
10.	Outside places for self and child from Lewes to London 9/9 extra /3	10	o
13.	Do. from London to Norwich	11	o
	Half price for Polly	5	6
15.	From Norwich to Filby outside 1/6 child /9 extras /3	2	6
	Breakfast dinner and supper 3 days on the road	10	o
	Expences in London July 3rd, 4th, 11th and 12th (say about)	10	o
	Things bought in London etc.	1 1	o

£5 4 o

Sally had travelled outside on the cheapest fare available and had not been extravagant, yet the total cost was a good deal more than Sylas had bargained for, and when the child unfortunately became a bone of contention between them, the housekeeping at Scratby was often as stormy as the cruel Norfolk weather. Sylas was not above getting his friends and neighbours to spy on Sally when he thought she was being too familiar with his manservant behind his back, and Sally cried bitterly when Sylas set off alone in the coach to London— not without some reason, for Sylas was highly susceptible to feminine charm and his acts of benevolence where quite unpredictable.

After leaving Norwich at midnight and stopping at Newmarket for breakfast, he was 'much struck with the beauty of a young lady of Norwich' travelling with him: 'her complexion a pretty brown enlivened with red, skin bluish, her eyes a most beautiful dark blue and have a most engaging sweetness, her fine arched eye-brows and long lashes a fine dark brown, her hair of the same colour, mouth of a proper size and lips vermilion, her hand small and nails exceedingly pretty'—in fact, a paragon, except that 'her shape was not equal to her face'. They dined together at the Crown at Epping and although he thought from her conversation that she was rather too fond of London and its diversions, Sylas shared her enthusiasm for the theatre and commended her good sense 'in liking a Play best'. He wanted very much to find out her name, but could get no opportunity of asking the maid who was travelling with her and could only gather that she was going on a visit to her sister, who was the wife of a Mr Hague, a merchant in London. When they reached the Eagle at Snaresbrook, Mr Hague's chariot—one of the handsomest Sylas had ever seen, 'with a pair of fine nagtail bays and two very genteel servants'—was waiting to carry her to his country house at Watten on the Forest. Luckily Sylas saw her name, 'Miss Scott', written on the side of her small caravan trunk when it was taken out of the coach; but her going away 'shocked his spirits exceedingly' and he was very upset because Mr Hague's servants did not pull off their hats or show her any great respect.

In London, dining with a gentleman from Norwich, Sylas probed him for information about the Scotts and discovered that the young lady's father was a well-to-do weaver of some importance in the town. The thought of her pretty hands and her vermilion lips filled his waking hours, and a fortnight later, when he returned to Norwich in the coach, he learnt that the elderly lady travelling with him was a distant relation of the Scotts. This was most exciting and for quite a time he forgot his queasy stomach, though he could not summon enough courage to question his companion directly and did not quite know whether to be pleased or not when she told him that Miss Scott was 'a mighty clever woman'. Back in Norwich he made some more inquiries about the family, but when he returned to his own complicated household at Scratby, his resolution wavered and he finally decided not to pursue the charming young lady's acquaintance any further.

Perhaps it was just as well. Sally was a fiend when she was jealous and Sylas suffered terribly from his nerves. He hated travelling at night—he could not sleep and his eyes hurt him. Yet he travelled continuously between London, Norwich, Newcastle and Edinburgh, spending much more money than he could actually afford and finding to his dismay that a great many of the innkeepers had pretty girls for their daughters, who often tempted him into one of his acts of benevolence which he came to regret afterwards. At some of the inns he was annoyed because he thought the landlords failed to show a proper respect for the coach passengers, even to those who were 'really gentlemen and ladies in dress and behaviour', and it made him very angry when they expected more money

EXPEDITIOUS TRAVELLING

FROM

LONDON TO GLASGOW AND PORTPATRICK,

IN FOUR DAYS,

BY WAY OF CARLISLE AND DUMFRIES.

A NEW POST COACH sets out from the 'CROSS KEYS,' WOOD STREET, LONDON, *every evening* (Saturday excepted), and arrives at BECK'S COFFEE HOUSE, CARLISLE, in three days ; also sets out from BECK'S COFFEE HOUSE, CARLISLE, *on the same evening,* and arrives in three days at the 'CROSS KEYS,' LONDON. To accommodate passengers travelling northward and to Ireland A NEW POST COACH, which connects with the above, sets out from 'KING'S ARMS HOTEL,' CARLISLE, *every Tuesday and Thursday morning* at six o'clock for DUMFRIES; upon arrival of which at the 'GEORGE INN,' a DILIGENCE sets out for GLASGOW and another for PORTPATRICK. Also a DILIGENCE sets out from MR. BUCHANAN'S, the 'SARACEN'S HEAD,' GLASGOW, and another from MR. CAMPBELL'S, PORTPATRICK, *every Tuesday and Thursday morning* at four o'clock, to join the said DUMFRIES AND CARLISLE POST COACH, in which seats will be reserved for those travelling southward.

Each inside passenger from Carlisle to Glasgow or Portpatrick to pay £1 16s. 6d., and to be allowed ten pounds weight of luggage ; all above to pay 2d. per lb. Children on the lap to pay half-price. Insides from Carlisle to Dumfries to pay 11s. 8d.; outsides, 6s. 8d. Small parcels from Carlisle to Portpatrick or Glasgow to pay 1s. 6d. each ; all upwards of nine pounds to pay 2d. per pound Passengers taken up on the road to pay 4d. per mile in both the Coach and Diligence; and for outsides on the Coach 2½d. per mile. Insides from London to Glasgow, £3 6s. Ditto from Carlisle to Glasgow or Portpatrick, £1 16s. 6d. Total : London to Glasgow or Portpatrick, £5 2s. 6d.

Advertisement for the Fast Post Coach to Glasgow, 1779

from him than he was able to pay. Scottish inns 'shocked
his spirits exceedingly'; the White Horse in Edinburgh
was a dismal place and very dirty, and the George at
Dunbar 'the nastiest house on the road—it stank
horribly; meat, fowls etc were hung up in the passage'
and were evidently responsible for the bad odour.
English inns were more attractive; his favourite was the
Crown at Epping—perhaps because it reminded him of
his dinner there with Miss Scott.

After five years in Edinburgh, Sylas managed to
qualify as a doctor, but could never bring himself to
settle down there or anywhere else as a practitioner. He
disliked the Scottish capital; and his housekeeping there
with Sally was even more difficult than in Norfolk,
because they lived in lodgings and had to put up with
the malevolent curiosity of one mischief-making landlady after another, while Sally's frequent excursions in
the coach to Newcastle when she was pregnant caused
no end of worry and expense. Eventually Sylas decided
to marry her off to his servant, Jack Read, and to settle
them both in Newcastle, thus leaving himself more free
to indulge in his restless passion for roving about the
country; and in spite of the wear and tear of so much
continuous travelling, even with the pains in his stomach,
his bad eye-sight and his nervous disorders, he managed
to live to the age of ninety-nine, becoming a querulous,
ill-tempered crusty old bachelor of very limited means,
who spent his time writing begging letters to anyone of
importance he thought might assist him. He gave up
writing his journal in 1784—in the very year that a revolution in coach travel was set in motion by John Palmer
of Bath.

8

THE
MAIL-COACH
REVOLUTION

THE FIRST MAIL-COACH to run between Bristol, Bath
and London in August 1784 was a triumph of individual
foresight and enthusiasm over the lethargy and lack of
imagination of a Government department. Only a man of
great ability, with immense self-confidence, determination and drive, could have achieved what John Palmer
set out to do against the obstructive and hostile attitude
of the General Post Office. Without the support of
William Pitt, perhaps he would not have succeeded as
well as he did, yet the brilliant idea he conceived when
still in his thirties became an obsession with him and he
brought the single-mindedness and the passion of an
artist to bear upon his purpose. Proud, impatient of
fools and arrogant in his careless defiance of authority,
he believed in his own vision of a fast and reliable system
of transport over the roads radiating out of London to
all parts of the country and, without ever turning aside,
gave all his energy to the task of translating his vision
into reality.

He was born in Bath in 1742 when Beau Nash still reigned in the Pump Room and Ralph Allen, another reformer of the Post Office, was living at Prior Park. His father, a well-to-do brewer and spermaceti-merchant, had other commercial interests in the city as the owner of the Orchard Street Theatre and of a second theatre in Bristol. And it was with these interests, after a false start in his father's brewery and a disappointment in not being allowed to make the army his career, that young John Palmer became involved, proving his ability in his early twenties when his father sent him to London to negotiate a licence for the Orchard Street Theatre. Not a single playhouse in the provinces possessed this enviable privilege dating from the restoration of King Charles II and enjoyed by the three principal theatres in London, and, to anyone less dynamic than young Palmer, his mission would have looked hopeless from the start. Yet by lobbying the right people, by cutting through the red-tape of the Lord Chamberlain's Office and by using all the persistence and the persuasiveness at his command, this elegant and attractive young man succeeded where everyone else had failed. He came home with a royal licence in his pocket for both of his father's theatres and this at once raised them to the status of Covent Garden, Drury Lane and the King's Theatre in the Haymarket, not only in the eyes of the *beau monde* visiting the fashionable city of Bath, but for members of the theatrical profession seeking engagements outside London. The Orchard Street Theatre took the proud title of Theatre Royal and became the scene of Sarah Siddons's first triumph in tragedy and of innumerable plays performed by Garrick's great rival, Henderson, who acted there and in Bristol for several seasons.

To operate both theatres successfully with one company of actors meant a great deal of travelling about between Bath and Bristol. Mrs Siddons often complained of being exhausted when obliged to rehearse in Bath on a Monday before going on to act in Bristol on the same day, and then having to return to Bath after a drive of twelve miles, 'to represent some fatiguing part there' on the Tuesday evening. Palmer arranged for her to travel by post-chaise from one theatre to the other in the shortest possible time and with the least amount of strain on her nerves; but this was expensive, and it was even more expensive and difficult to bring actors down from London, or to get a prompt reply to any letters, contracts or other kind of mail sent by post from the West of England to the capital.

At this time when the stage-coach from London to Bath was taking only seventeen hours to accomplish the journey, the post still took anything up to three days to arrive at its destination—a maddening situation for anyone with John Palmer's instinctive desire for efficiency. Letters disguised as parcels or hidden in the pockets of the passengers were often secretly despatched to London by the coach, though it was strictly against the law to by-pass the regulations and defraud the revenue in this way. The Post Office, ever since its inauguration in the time of Henry VIII, had enjoyed an absolute monopoly in the carrying of letters to and from one point to another. Postboys, who could be of any age from sixteen to sixty and more often than not were quite elderly, rode off alone with the mail done up in a canvas bag and were supposed to travel at a rate of not less than six miles an hour. But they seldom kept to time, being constantly hindered by the weather or tempted to loiter at the posting-inns on the road where they changed horses and stayed to drink with the landlord, sometimes setting off so befuddled they were no match for the rascally highwaymen intent on robbing the mail. They were defenceless, anyway, since the Post Office did not consider it necessary for them to carry a pistol or a

fowling-piece and anyone armed with a weapon of any
sort could easily overpower them and get away with their
bags without much fear of being apprehended. Mail
robberies were, in fact, so frequent that the Post Office
calmly advised people to cut their bank-notes in half
before sending them off by post, so that news of the safe
arrival of one half could be obtained before the second
half was despatched to join it.

Such inept proceedings rankled in the energetic mind
of John Palmer and it was not long before he saw a
solution to the problem that was vexing nearly everyone
except their Lordships, the Postmasters-General themselves. Why should the mail not be sent by a fast coach
with an armed guard to protect it and four passengers,
whose fares would help to pay the cost? Why not, indeed?
The idea was so simple it should have been obvious to
all concerned—but it was not. Years of sluggish
behaviour among the officials in the Post Office had
closed their minds to anything new in the way of
progress. They were perfectly satisfied with what they
were doing and did not believe it could be done any
better, and they were jealous of the power and the
privilege they had inherited from the past, when 'post
haste' written on the front of a letter really meant something and the King's Post was adequate for the needs of
the country. Two peers of the realm filled the combined
office of the Postmasters-General and beneath them a
horde of underlings called District Surveyors managed
the correspondence of the nation. They did not look
kindly on the brilliant plan Palmer presented to them.
For one thing they were inside, and he was not—and
they resented anyone bold enough to criticize the way
they managed their affairs. For another the idea of
having an armed guard to go with the mails shocked their
sense of decorum. What if the guard should actually
shoot someone trying to rob the mails? Would the Post

Office be held responsible for murder? It was really much safer, they decided, to cut bank-notes in half than to risk so grave an accusation—and without more ado they turned the plan down, believing, no doubt, that they would hear no more of Mr Palmer.

But they were wrong in thinking that Palmer could be so easily defeated. Instead he worked still harder on his plan. Having abandoned his interests in the theatre, he travelled all over the country, getting to know the innkeepers who horsed the coaches down the road, inquiring into the way they conducted their business and finding out what it cost in time and money. Before he had finished there was nothing he did not know about coach travel from one end of England to the other, and what was more important, he knew that William Pitt was in favour of his plan. Pitt, as Chancellor of the Exchequer in the Shelburne administration, had at once realized its possibilities and, as soon as he was returned to power in the spring of 1784, he acted promptly. Calling a conference of their Lordships and the district postmasters, he listened to all their objections, which according to Palmer were enough 'to furnish three large volumes', and then, with his supreme authority as Prime Minister and First Lord of the Treasury, he overruled the lot. The plan, he insisted, must be given a trial—at Palmer's own expense—and its success or its failure judged by the results.

This was the moment the ex-theatrical impresario had been waiting for; his two years of intensive preparation were not wasted. Yet there were last-minute difficulties which had to be overcome, and a man with less determination might well have found them insuperable. Some coach proprietors and innkeepers who horsed the stage-coaches down the Bath Road were indignant and afraid of the competition they would have to meet if the mail-coach was a success. Others more willing to assist had to

7

be found, with good stables and a staff capable of changing the horses with the least possible delay: two in Bath, one at Marlborough, another at Thatcham and the fifth in London at the Swan with Two Necks. Passengers had to be reassured that 'both the Guards and the Coachmen (who will be likewise armed) have given ample Security for their Conduct to the Proprietors, so that those Ladies and Gentlemen who may please to honour them with their Encouragement, may depend on every Respect and Attention', but nothing whatever was said about the time schedule being kept 'if God permit'. Williams in Bath, Fromont at Thatcham and Wilson in London had no loophole, and the man behind them could only wait and see how they discharged their obligation.

He was not disappointed. The first mail-coach, leaving Bristol at four in the afternoon and travelling all night with an armed guard and four inside passengers, turned into the yard of the Swan with Two Necks in Lad Lane precisely at eight o'clock the next morning. The mail-bags were safe and the passengers had spent one hour less on the road than if they had travelled by the stage-coach. They had moreover a sense of security they had never known before; the guard, whose name was Carter, sat by the coachman with his blunderbuss across his knees and even in the small hours of the morning no highwayman appeared from the thickets of Hounslow Heath to challenge the fast-moving vehicle.

Within a very short time the mail-coach idea had caught on with the public as a safe and convenient way of travelling about as well as a means of having their correspondence more speedily delivered. Palmer, disregarding the animosity of the Post Office, still intriguing against him with all the cunning of a long-established bureaucracy, greatly extended the service to cover a very wide area. His capacity for organizing the whole complicated system down to the smallest detail was never in doubt, but by 1786 he had reached the end of his private financial resources and Pitt, realizing the supreme value of his service to the state, created a special post for him with the title of Surveyor and Comptroller General to the Post Office at a salary of £1,500 a year with a bonus of 2½ per cent on all Post Office revenue above £300,000. This was rather less than Palmer had been hoping for: he was inside the citadel at last and had nothing much to complain of financially; but as Comptroller he was subordinate to the authority of their Lordships, the Postmasters-General, and it was not long before he came up against the pettifogging interference of Lord Walsingham, who, unlike his colleague, Lord Cartaret, had an insatiable appetite for inquiring into every branch of the daily activities of the department he had been appointed to rule.

Two such men as Walsingham and Palmer, each convinced of his own superiority, were bound to quarrel sooner or later. Walsingham had the sharp, pedantic mind of a lawyer and failed entirely or made no attempt to understand the more volatile disposition of Palmer, and Palmer had every reason to believe that he alone was capable of running the organization he had created by his own enterprise. A wiser man would have paid lip-service to authority and still have mastered the situation. Palmer had no cunning of that sort and no humility, nothing of the place-hunter or the lackey in his make-up; instead he was wildly and madly indiscreet, to the extent of writing discreditable things about Lord Walsingham in the confidential letters he addressed to his deputy and friend, Charles Bonnor. He trusted Bonnor whom he had known first as an actor in Bath and Bristol, and for once in his life his judgment let him down; for the ex-actor was busily intriguing behind his back and as time went on became so involved in his own malpractice, that the only way he could see of saving himself was to expose his friend, the Comptroller General. This he did most effectively by taking the confidential letters he had never destroyed to their Lordships, the Postmasters-General. Even Pitt, in the face of such shocking evidence of Palmer's attempt to discredit Lord Walsingham, stated with a freedom and a gaiety that were nothing short of libellous, had no alternative but to acquiesce in the dismissal of the Comptroller General, though he showed his gratitude for Palmer's astonishing achievement by granting him a pension of £3,000 a year, and the mail-coach system was by then so firmly established, even the Postmasters-General had been compelled to accept its overwhelming superiority to all other methods of communication.

In six years Palmer had changed the whole pattern of travelling in Britain. By the time he was dismissed, the first rather ramshackle mail-coach from Bath had given way to a specially designed vehicle with a boot at the back framed to the body and a seat for the guard, whose feet were firmly planted on top of the locked mail-box. Lighter and more elegant than a stage-coach it was painted maroon and black with scarlet wheels, and the doors were decorated with the Royal Arms. The emblems of the four orders of knighthood—the Garter the Bath, the Thistle and St Patrick—were picked out in colour on the upper panels of the body, and on the fore-boot where the coachman sat was the cipher of the reigning monarch. One coachmaker in Millbank, by the name of Vidler, had the monopoly of building and supplying the coaches to the contractors who horsed them down the road, and he was also responsible for their maintenance. Every coach that came into London in the morning, bespattered with mud and thick with dust, was immediately taken back to the works at Millbank to be cleaned and greased and overhauled before being put on the road again the same afternoon, and more than one was kept in reserve in case of accident.

But the mail-coach of the seventeen-nineties was hung very high and not everyone approved of its design. Matthew Boulton, himself an engineer and a pioneer among those who were shortly to transform the world with the new dynamic power of the steam engine, complained of the springs when he travelled from London to Exeter in 1798. 'I had the most disagreeable journey I ever experienced the night after I left you, owing to the new improved coach,' he wrote to a friend, 'a vehicle loaded with iron trappings and the greatest complication of unmechanical contrivances jumbled together that I have ever witnessed. The coach swings sideways with a sickly sway, without any vertical spring; the point of suspense bearing upon an arch called a spring, though it is nothing of the sort. The severity of the jolting occasioned me such disorder that I was obliged to stop at Axminster and go to bed very ill. However, I was able to proceed next day in a post-chaise. The landlady at the London Inn at Exeter assured me that the passengers who arrived every night were in general so ill that they were obliged to go supper-less to bed; and unless they go back to the old-fashioned coach, hung a little lower, the mail-coaches will lose all their custom.'

Matthew Boulton and the landlady at Exeter were mistaken. Travellers, especially the well-off merchants and their wives and the commissioned officers in the army and the navy or those who belonged to the new professional classes, enjoyed the speed and the reliability of the mails, even if they had no appetite for supper when they arrived at their journey's end. The mails were more exclusive than the common stage-coach and more expensive. It cost Tom Moore, the Irish poet and song-writer, three and a half guineas to travel up to London

from Chester when he first came over from Ireland in
1799, but he was impatient to arrive at his destination,
having never been to London before, and although he
met a very doubtful gentleman in the coach and was still
very young and untried in the ways of the world, he
managed to evade being tricked by his companion and to
give himself great credit for accomplishing his first
English journey in such style.

Only one outside passenger sitting by the coachman
was allowed on the mails at this time, and the four
inside passengers were prepared to pay a high price for
the convenience of arriving on schedule. The guard
carried a time-piece locked inside a leather pouch, which
marked the exact hours and minutes taken from one
stage to the next and could not be tampered with; and
the coachmen, if they were running late, considered it a
point of honour to make up the time as they went along.
One great advantage was that every other vehicle on the
road had to give way to the mails and they were exempt
from the tolls which delayed and annoyed every other
sort of traveller. When the mail came within sight of the
turnpike, the guard took out his horn and began to wake
the dead with its high-sounding flourish, and the toll-
keepers jerked themselves out of their sleep just in time
to fling the gates open to let the mail through.

On the long-distance runs more than one coachman
took up the reins, but the guard, who was paid by the
Post Office, travelled the whole way with the coach and
was responsible for the way-bill where every detail of the
journey and all the passengers names had to be entered.
His first duty was to get the mails safely to their destination. As Palmer had foreseen, the very fact that he was
armed acted as a deterrent and mail robberies declined
immediately. If the guard forgot or did not take the
trouble to lock the mail-box, it was sometimes rifled when
his back was turned at one of the halts on the road, but

thieves thought twice before daring to hold up the coach when it was travelling at speed through the night and from that point of view the passengers could rely on a safe and pleasant journey. It was disconcerting, however, if the guard got bored and aimed a pot-shot at the game he saw by the wayside or simply fired off his blunderbuss for fun. Palmer's successor, Thomas Hasker, who became Superintendent of the Mail-Coaches in 1792, was constantly issuing directives to the guards on this question, though he was more concerned about their good behaviour and the example they set to others than with the passengers' apprehension of some untoward accident occurring when the guard put his finger on the trigger.

Passengers also had to accept the fact that if the weather was exceptionally bad, the guard might have to abandon them altogether to set off on one or more of the coach-horses with the mail-bags strung across his shoulders. In the terrible winter of 1799 when it snowed heavily all through January and February, many a traveller going north found himself stuck in a blind white world with no hope of proceeding any farther and his choice lay between freezing to death inside the half-buried vehicle or attempting to fight his way on foot through the shoulder-high drifts to a more convenient shelter. Several of the mail-coaches were actually still missing by the end of April and the subject of one of Hasker's most impassioned appeals to the guards, wherein he begged them to inform him at once of 'the exact place where they are, either in *Barn*, *Field*, *Yard* or *Coach-house*, and the Condition they are in, and if they have Seats, Rugs and Windows complete'. The condition the passengers might be in did not apparently concern his active mind, though to have come through such an ordeal must have shaken the nerves of the most indomitable traveller and if the seats and the rugs were missing, the passengers could hardly be blamed for availing themselves of the only comfort to be found in the cold at dead of night somewhere on the Great North Road.

Yet everyone who travelled by the mails had reason to be grateful to Hasker for his meticulous attention to the smallest item concerned with their smooth running. His office was no sinecure. He worked unceasingly to perfect the instrument Palmer had designed and he was a man of infinite pains who managed to organize his affairs without ever losing his instinctive understanding of human nature. Though he could be very severe with the guards, he was always ready to give them the benefit of the doubt and to warn them first before taking action against them. In one letter he addressed to them he wrote: 'Half my time is employed in receiving and answering Letters of Complaint from Passengers respecting improper Conduct and impertinent Language of Guards. I am very sorry to dismiss sober honest Men, but I must have Civility also, and when you behave impertinently to Passengers, they find out some other Error to couple their Complaint with, that nothing less than Dismission can succeed. This plainly shows how circumspect Guards should be in their Behaviour, and I must insist that you conduct yourself so properly in all your Words and Actions as to prevent Complaints.'

The Superintendent evidently had the unenviable task of deciding whether the passengers' complaints were justified or not and being somewhat biased in favour of the service, very often he decided that they were not. Those who wished to linger over their breakfast or their dinner at the inns along the road were a great nuisance. If they wanted to take advantage of the speed of the mails, they would have to accept the time allowed for meals even at the cost of suffering some inconvenience— or so it seemed to Hasker when writing to one of his mail-guards in August 1796. 'Stick to your bill,' he advised, 'and never mind what passengers say respecting over time. Is it not the fault of the Landlord to keep them so long? Some day when you have waited a considerable time, suppose 5 or 8 minutes longer than is allowed by the Bill, drive away and leave them behind, only take care that you have a witness that you called them out two or three times—then let them go forward how they can.'

This was stern advice, but 'no lenity' as Hasker phrased it, could be allowed: 'to keep the Duty regular' was his first consideration. Horse-keepers who failed to have fresh horses already standing in the road when the coach arrived even in the middle of the night, so that no more than five minutes would be needed to change them, were guilty of grave misconduct. Guards and coachmen, tempted by thirsty passengers willing to give them an extra tip, were warned that 'Stopping at Alehouses on the Road between Stage and Stage under Pretence of watering horses, but in Reality to drink, have been found very detrimental to the Service', and dilatory landlords, hoping to get more out of the mail-coach passengers by deliberately delaying their meals, were charged with gross negligence. Yet even Hasker sometimes had to turn a blind eye on the guards' practice of carrying fish and game in the mail-box and while he suggested that 'to load the roof of the Coach with huge heavy Baskets would be setting a bad example to other Coaches', he did admit that 'such a thing as a turtle tied on the roof directed to any Gentleman once or twice a year might pass un-noticed'.

Perhaps Hasker himself had a taste for turtle soup. Without Palmer's spectacular genius, but with infinite patience and no small amount of pride in the complex organization he held together by his own exertions and the help of two underpaid and overworked deputies, he was a gift to their Lordships, the Postmasters-General.

He was always respectful, though not without a certain
underlying firmness in his dealings with them, and they
had the sense to trust him. He handled the contractors
who horsed the mails with the utmost skill, and if
anything went seriously wrong anywhere, he was not
content to sit in his office in the hope of it being put right;
he took the first available coach to wherever the trouble
happened to be and made a personal investigation on the
spot, interviewing the passengers as well as the guards,
the coachmen and the innkeepers. By the time he retired
in 1817, after twenty-five years of selfless devotion to
his work, no one, inside or outside the Post Office, even
thought of questioning the supremacy of the mail-coach
system over every other kind of transport on the road,
and for the first time in history people were able to
travel about Britain with ease and security.

9

THE GLORY

OF

MOTION

THE MAIL-COACHES brought a new glamour and excitement to the road. 'The finest sight in the metropolis,' Hazlitt declared, 'is the setting off of the mailcoaches from Piccadilly. The horses paw the ground and are impatient to be gone, as if conscious of the precious burden they convey. There is a peculiar secrecy and dispatch, significant and full of meaning, in all the proceedings concerning them. Even the outside passengers [three were allowed by this time] have an erect and supercilious air, as if proof against the accidents of the journey; in fact, it seems indifferent whether they are to encounter the summer's heat or the winter's cold, since they are borne through the air on a winged chariot. The mail-carts drive up and the transfer of packages is made, and at a given signal off they start, bearing the irrevocable scrolls that give wings to thought and that bind or sever hearts for ever. How we hate the Putney and Brentford stages that draw up when they are gone! Some persons think the sublimest object in nature is a

ship launched on the bosom of the ocean; but give me
for my private satisfaction the mail-coaches that pour
down Piccadilly of an evening, tear up the pavement and
devour the way before them to Land's End.'

Such a superb spectacle appealed to the romantic
spirit in Hazlitt and fired his imagination, and as for
travelling by coach, no one knew better than he what it
could lead to. The failure of his first marriage and his
unhappy love affair with Sarah Walker had been enough
to drive all ideas of romance out of his desperate mind,
yet it was in a coach on the Great North Road that he
first met Isabella Bridgewater and found her sym-
pathetic. As she was a widow with £300 a year and
professed to be already in love with his writings, their
acquaintance ripened very quickly into a marriage which,
however, only lasted for three years and brought little
happiness to either of them.

Thomas de Quincey, equally romantic and even more
imaginative than Hazlitt when under the spell of his
addiction to laudanum, declared that the mail-coaches
first revealed to him 'the glory of motion'. Looking back
to his student days at Oxford, he remembered 'the
grand effects for the eye between lamp-light and the
darkness upon solitary roads, and the animal beauty and
power so often displayed in the class of horses selected
for the mail service'. For him and his young friends the
outside seats had an advantage they would not forego
even for the snobbish assumption that outsiders were of a
lower class than the passengers travelling inside. 'The
higher price we would willingly have paid,' he wrote,
'but not the price connected with the condition of riding
inside; which condition we pronounced insufferable. The
air, the freedom of prospect, the proximity to the horses,
the elevation of the seat, these were what we required;
but above all the certain anticipation of purchasing
occasional opportunities of driving.' After a searching

inquiry into the true quality and valuation of the different apartments about the mail, they decided that 'the roof of the coach, which by some weak men had been called the attics, and by some the garrets, was in reality the drawing-room; in which drawing-room the box was the chief ottoman or sofa; whilst it appeared that the *inside*, which had been regarded as the only room tenantable by gentleman, was, in fact, the coal-cellar in disguise'.

This well-considered conclusion having been reached, de Quincey never lost an opportunity of obtaining his favourite seat on the box by the coachmen when going down from Oxford on the Gloucester or the Holyhead mail: and from this seat the sensation of speed to anyone of his excitable temperament was intoxicating. 'We heard our speed,' he declared, 'we saw it, we felt it as thrilling; and this speed was not the product of blind insensate agencies, that had no sympathy to give, but was incarnated in the fiery eyeballs in the noblest among brutes, in his dilated nostril, spasmodic muscles and thunder-beating hoofs.'

The sound of the thunder-beating hoofs and of the guard blowing his long horn rang through the countryside and gave new life to the towns and the villages on the road. Like a meteor in the sky, the mail-coach brightened the lives of hundreds of people who never even thought of travelling on it, providing them with a thrilling spectacle of speed and smartness belonging to the great world outside their parish boundaries. Labourers looked up from their work in the fields and ploughmen paused to stare in wonder and surprise. Villagers ran to their windows to wave or gathered on the green to watch the passengers riding high on top of the elegant equipage. They set their clocks by the mail, so regular was its appearance, and wherever it stopped for the horses to be changed or the passengers to snatch some refreshment, they surrounded it excitedly, eager above all to hear what news the travellers brought with them.

De Quincey, in an ecstasy of patriotic fervour, said that it was worth paying down five years of life for the privilege of an outside place on a mail-coach carrying down to the country the first tidings of victory in the Napoleonic wars. He described the mails assembled on parade outside the General Post Office in Lombard Street, drawn up in double file the whole length of the street: 'the absolute perfection of all the appointments about the carriages and their harness, their strength, their brilliant cleanliness, their beautiful simplicity . . .'. And on the night following a victory, even more was added to this splendid display. Horses, men, carriages, all were dressed in laurels and flowers, oak-leaves and ribbons. The guards in their royal scarlet liveries wore laurel leaves in their hats, the coachmen, scorning a top-coat, flowers in their buttonholes, and the usual reserve of the gentlemen travelling as passengers melted away in the sudden friendliness they showed towards everyone, even to the stable-boys and ostlers with whom on any ordinary night they would never have thought of exchanging a single word unless it was to command some extra attention. 'One heart, one pride, one glory connected every man by the transcendent bond of his national blood'; and while the spectators shouted and cheered, the Post Office servants called out 'the great ancestral names of cities known to history through a thousand years—Lincoln, Winchester, Portsmouth, Gloucester, Oxford, Bristol, Manchester, York, Newcastle, Edinburgh, Glasgow, Perth, Sterling, Aberdeen— expressing the grandeur of the empire by the antiquity of its towns . . .'. Then there was 'the thunder of lids locked down upon the mail-bags', the signal for drawing off—and away the horses bounded with a trampling of

hoofs to the cheers of the multitude, while 'the half-
slumbering consciousness that all night long and all the
next day many of these mails, like fire racing along a
train of gunpowder, would be kindling at every instant
new successions of burning joy', had, according to de
Quincey, 'an effect of multiplying the victory itself'.

Passengers on these occasions enjoyed an almost royal
progress through the country. No sooner had the guard
sounded his horn, than a hundred eyes appeared at all
the windows to rejoice at the sight of the be-ribboned
and laurel-decked mails sweeping along the road with
news of a great victory for Wellington and his armies.
The young and the old, even at night when the mail-
coach lamps made a flare-path in the summer darkness,
ran out to cheer and to wave, and the passengers were
caught up in a great surge of enthusiasm which drew the
country together as never before. No wonder de Quincey
never forgot his journey. Against overwhelming odds and
often alone, after long years of struggle, the people of
Britain had won their freedom and not for the first, or
for the last time, had liberated the world from tyranny.

Tom Moore, with Irish perversity, was one of the very
few who continued to admire Napoleon and to sound a
sour note in the midst of all the rejoicing. 'I arrived very
tired on Saturday evening,' he wrote of his journey home
to Mayfield Cottage in June 1814, 'not the less so for
meeting with very unexpected honours from the fools of
Derby, who came out to meet us about a mile from the
town (on account of the confirmation of Peace) with
ribbons, oak-leaves etc, took the horses from the mail
and pulled us thro the town. . . . The only thing that
amused me in the whole business was an idea that struck
me of buying a *whiskered mask*, before we came to Derby,
which I made a man in the mail (who had an odd sort of
black tufted travelling cap) put on and he hurraed like a
Don Cossack out of the windows.'

It was just as well that Moore and de Quincey were not fellow passengers; both held the strongest opinions and when travellers started arguing with each other, they could make a journey together far from pleasant. De Quincey allowed his enthusiasm for the mails to bias his mind against the stage-coaches, which ran in competition with them and were now much faster and more reliable than they had ever been. 'Once I remember being on the box of the Holyhead mail between Shrewsbury and Oswestry,' he wrote, 'when a tawdry thing from Birmingham, some "Tally-ho" or "Highflyer", all flaunting with green and gold, came up alongside of us. What a contrast to our royal simplicity of form and colour in this plebeian wretch! The single ornament on our dark ground of chocolate colour was the mighty shield of the imperial arms. . . whilst the beast from Birmingham, our green-and-gold friend from false, fleeting, perjured Brummagem, had as much writing and painting on its sprawling flanks as would have puzzled a decipherer from the tombs of Luxor.' For a time the two coaches ran side by side along the road at a break-neck pace and de Quincey was in a frenzy of indignation at the Birmingham coach even daring to challenge the superiority of the mail, let alone attempting to pass it; then the mail-coachman unloosed his royal horses 'like cheetahs or hunting-leopards', and threw the offending stage-coach into the rear and out of the race altogether. But de Quincey's excitement over the achievement of the mail-coach was not shared by his fellow passenger, a Welsh rustic, who disliked the idea of racing—it frightened him—and was rather sorry for the loser.

Racing could be very frightening indeed. It depended on the art of the coachman and the passengers were entirely at his mercy. If they were regular travellers, they could at once assess whether he was experienced or not —and if he was not, they had some reason to be afraid.

Passengers, paying half-price, rode in the
basket, or the 'conveniency behind'

(Radio Times Hulton Picture Library)

BIRMINGHAM
STAGE-COACH,

In Two *Days* and a half; begins *May* the
24th, '1731.

SET Sout from the *Swan-Inn* in *Birmingham*,
every *Monday* at fix a Clock in the Morning,
through *Warwick*, *Banbury* and *Alesbury*,
to the *Red Lion Inn* in *Alderfgate ftreet*, *London*,
every *Wednefday* Morning: And returns from
the faid *Red Lion Inn* every *Thurfday* Morning
at five a Clock the fame Way to the *Swan-Inn*
in *Birmingham* every *Saturday*, at 21 Shillings
each Paffenger, and 18 Shillings from *Warwick*,
who has liberty to carry 14 Pounds in Weight,
and all above to *pay One Penny a Pound*,
            Perform d (if God permit)

By Nicholas Rothwell.

The Weekly Waggon fets out every *Tuefday* from the *Nagg's-Head* in
Birmingham, to the Red Lion Inn aforefaid, every *Saturday*, and returns
from the faid Inn every *Monday*, to the *Nagg's-Head* in *Birmingham* every
Thurfday.

Note. *By the faid* Nicholas Rothwell *at* Warwick, *all Perfons may be fur-
nifhed with a 'By-Coach' Chariot. Chaife or Hearfe, with a Mourning Coach
and able Horfes, to any Part of Great Britain, at reafonable Rates: And
alfo Saddle Horfes to be had*

Coach loading up in a country inn yard —
Hogarth, 1747

(Radio Times Hulton Picture Library)

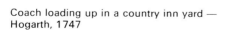

Old coaching bills: York — 1706,
Birmingham — 1731

(Radio Times Hulton Picture Library)

YORK Four Days
Stage-Coach.

Begins on Friday the 12th of April. 1706.

ALL that are defirous to pafs from *London* to *York*,
or from *York* to *London*, or any other Place
on that Road; Let them Repair to the *Black Swan* in
Holbourn in *London*, and to the *Black Swan* in *Coney
ftreet* in *York*.

At both which Places. they may be received in a
Stage Coach every *Monday, Wednefday* and *Friday*,
which performs the whole Journey in Four Days, (*if
God permits*,) And fets forth at Five in the Morning.

And returns from *York* to *Stamford* in two days,
and from *Stamford* by *Huntington* to *London* in two
days more. And the like Stages on their return.

Allowing each Paffenger 14 , weight, and all above 3d a Pound.

Performed By ⎨ *Benjamin Kingman,*
Henry Harrifon,
Walter Bayne's

Alfo this gives Notice that Newcaftle Stage Coach, fets
out from York, every Monday, and Friday, and
from Newcaftle every Monday and Friday.

The first mail-coach from Bath to London, — 1784

(Photo: John Freeman)

'Flying' coach at the Bell Savage Inn, where Parson Woodforde 'was bit terribly by the Buggs'

(Radio Times Hulton Picture Library)

Mail-coach travelling at night — James Pollard

(Solomon & Whitehead Ltd.)

Stage-coach with the news of peace, — James Pollard 1814

The 'Star', leaving La Belle
Sauvage for Cambridge —
1835

(Radio Times Hulton Picture
Library)

Royal Mails preparing to leave the Swan with Two Necks in Lad Lane — James Pollard

(Mansell Collection)

Passengers walking up a steep hill in Derbyshire — James Pollard

The 'Comet' fast coach from London to Brighton — James Pollard, 1822

Patent safety coach, the 'Sovereign' —
James Pollard

(Photo; John Freeman)

Passengers in the snow — H. Alken

(Radio Times Hulton Picture Library)

Breakfast at the Bull Inn, Redbourn — James Pollard

Mail-coach in a flood — James Pollard

Gurney's steam carriage — 1828

(Radio Times Hulton Picture Library)

The quality of the horses had greatly improved and the practice of changing them at shorter stages meant they were always fresh with much more energy and power in them, and consequently more difficult to handle. The old type of hard-drinking, hard-swearing coachman who flogged his team along with cruel persistence, was dying out in favour of the more spruce and well-mannered driver, who knew exactly how to get the best out of his 'cattle', and the comfort of travelling depended a great deal on whether the horses were a well-matched team driven by an expert hand.

It depended also on the way the coach was loaded. Too much luggage piled on the roof or badly disposed, disturbed the balance of the vehicle, so that it swayed and lurched with a perilous motion and seemed likely to overturn going round a bend. Regulations about the number of persons and the amount of baggage allowed on each coach were often overlooked, as on the occasion when there were 'thirty-four persons in and about the Hertford coach', which not surprisingly broke down by one of the traces giving way, one outside passenger being killed on the spot and a woman traveller having both legs broken, while everyone else was severely shaken. A good coachman always kept a sharp eye on the loading of his vehicle, and, following the example of the mails, the bigger and more important stage-coach proprietors supplied a guard, whose business it was to assist the coachman and to take care of the passengers. The hit or miss timing which had suited travellers well enough in the past, was no longer acceptable and since more people than ever were travelling, the booking-offices, mostly centred at the inns from which the coaches departed, were kept busy night and day.

The Rev. James Woodforde always went into Norwich from Weston Parsonage two or three days before he intended going on a journey and booked his tickets at

8

the Angel, paying down half the fare before he started
and the balance at the end of his trip. He was a somewhat anxious traveller and one who found going on a
journey a considerable undertaking, especially when it
meant taking his niece, Nancy, and his servant, Will
Coleman, all the way to Somerset to stay with his Sister
Pounsett at Cole. Having booked two inside places for
himself and Nancy and one outside for Will, he was very
busy packing up all the morning of 28th May 1782,
before they set out at five o'clock in a chaise for Norwich.
At the Angel they drank tea with a friend of theirs, Mr
du Quesne, who was also travelling to London, and it
cost them 2s. 6d. The two inside places in the coach cost
£1 16s. and the outside place for Will 10s. 6d., and 'the
extraordinary weight of Luggage' they took with them
in excess of the 14 lb. each passenger was allowed,
amounted to 8s. 6d. at 1½d. per pound. This was a good
deal more than Woodforde had expected, but as they
intended spending the greater part of the summer in
Somerset and Nancy liked pretty clothes, they could not
very well do with less.

They entered the coach at nine o'clock in the evening
and travelled all night—'I thank God safe and well', the
parson wrote in his diary. Breakfast at Sudbury cost them
2s. 6d., and as there were two coachmen on the run, tips
to each of them added up to another 4s. The coach was
full with six inside and a number of outside passengers,
all with a considerable amount of baggage, but it reached
London on time at two o'clock in the afternoon and
Woodforde was pleased that Nancy bore her journey very
well. They did not like the Swan with Two Necks in Lad
Lane where the coach put up, so they hired a hackney
coach to take them to the Bell Savage on Ludgate Hill
instead, and after supper they were all very glad to get
to bed, being very tired.

Woodforde 'was bit terribly by the Buggs' in the night,

but they did not apparently wake him and he thought the Bell Savage 'a very good House'. It was now kept by 'very civil People', called Barton, and had a high reputation among the London inns, though at about this time, a gentleman had his 'Caravan Trunk covered in Paper' stolen from there, and as it contained 'a light coloured cloth Coat lined with silk of the same Colour, a blue silk Waistcoat with spangled Lace, a black silk Waistcoat, two pairs of black silk Breeches, a dozen Shirts marked G.R., eleven Stocks the same Mark and other Apparel', it was quite a wardrobe to lose. Perhaps Woodforde was more careful about keeping an eye on his baggage. For bed and breakfast for his entire party, he paid £1 15s., which was reasonable enough, and one great advantage was that the Salisbury coach which they wanted to take in the evening, left from the yard of the Bell Savage so they did not have to hire another hackney coach to take them and their luggage across London.

During the day they did some sight-seeing, walking through St James's Park and going to the Tower to see the wild beasts and the armour. Then Nancy did some shopping at a smart milliner's in Covent Garden, where she bought '3 dressed Caps . . . with about 10 Yards of Ribband besides, and a small Paper Caravan' to pack them in. The parson found time to take 'a Peep into St Paul's' and to go to a barber in the Strand to have his wig dressed, and then at ten o'clock in the evening they got into the Salisbury coach.

Like the Norwich coach, it was full and the two inside seats at a guinea each were double the price of the out-side seat occupied by Will Coleman; but the luggage which should have been more expensive, only cost 6s. 6d. —perhaps Nancy's new caps and ribbons did not weigh enough to matter. Breakfast at Whitchurch cost 2s. 6d. and tips another 4s., but at Salisbury there was only

time for 'a running Dinner' before they got into a post-
chaise for Hindon, where they arrived at six o'clock and
got another chaise to take them on to Stourton, where
they changed into a third chaise, which finally brought
them to Cole by ten o'clock at night. The last part of the
journey, with uncle and niece travelling in the chaises
and Will mounted on a hired horse, was the most
expensive—it cost £2 6s. And by then Woodforde was
'terribly swelled in the face and hands by the Buggs',
but his Sister Pounsett, as he always called her, was
delighted to see him.

Several members of the Woodforde family lived in the
surrounding district: the parson's two brothers, John
and Heighes, who was Nancy's father, and another sister,
Sister White, and they all had sons and daughters who
made life gay and amusing for Nancy. She did not like
going back to Norfolk at all. She missed the company of
her brothers and sisters and cousins, and often found
living at the parsonage with her uncle rather dreary.
'Nancy very discontented of late and runs out against
living in such a dull Place,' he wrote in his diary. 'My
niece making me uneasy by continually complaining of
the dismal life she leads at Weston Parsonage for want of
being more out in Company and having more at Home . . . .'
It was not very easy for either of them. Woodforde
needed a housekeeper and was not ungenerous to her, but
Nancy was young and had very indifferent health, which
was enough to make anyone feel depressed. She dosed
herself with rhubarb and Dr James's powders and was
really very good-tempered when her uncle fussed about
his own health and got his feet wet walking to church.

Four years elapsed before they again journeyed down
to Somerset. This time Nancy's brother Bill, who was
in the navy, travelled with them, and in London, where
they stayed as usual at the Bell Savage, the two young
people gave their uncle the slip and walked out in the

evening by themselves, which upset him very much. The next day, however, they all dined at the 13 Cantons at Charing Cross on beef *à-la-mode*, which was very good, and Woodforde, obviously trying to please his niece and to make up for the dull life she led at home, bought her a very expensive pair of gauze gloves at Charlesworth's, a stylish haberdashers in Covent Garden, besides paying for her to have 'her Hair full dressed' at Smith's in the Strand. They saw the Royal Mews and the King's cream-coloured horses and Nancy sat in the King's state coach; then they all went to the Circus at St George's Fields one night and to a play at the Haymarket Theatre the next, not getting to bed until after midnight. Woodforde 'sat up in a great Chair all night' with his feet on the bed, without taking his clothes off, and by this uncomfortable stratagem, was not 'so terribly pestered with Buggs'.

But having booked to go on down to Somerset via Bath, there was very nearly a terrible disaster owing to the unreliability of Nancy's nautical brother, who had gone off somewhere with a friend of his and by seven o'clock had failed to reappear. 'Nancy and self got into the Bath Coach, and were just setting out, after some time waiting for Bill, when he luckily arrived,' the parson wrote afterwards, 'but it was enough to make one very mad, and he was obliged to leave some things behind him.' This coach was called the 'Balloon Coach', on account of its travelling so fast, and it did in fact beat the mail-coach on the run down to the fashionable west-country city. It carried four inside passengers and a guard on top and, being very light, was drawn by two horses instead of four—altogether a very elegant turn-out and a high-class mode of travelling.

Nancy had a wonderful time at Cole until the middle of August, when she was taken ill 'with something of the Ague'—and she was still not very well when she travelled back to Norfolk with her uncle at the beginning of

October. At Hindon, on the way to Salisbury, they were
obliged 'to bait the Horses' as they could get no chaise
on, but they were not alone in being held up—they found
'Mr Pitt, the prime Minister in the same Dilemma . . .
all the Horses at the inn being engaged', and when they
did get away, they reached Salisbury very late in the
evening. The coach for London left at five o'clock the
next morning and was thirteen hours on the road, but a
handsome young officer in the guards and a sensible old
gentleman from Stockbridge travelled with them and
helped to pass the time away.

   They stayed a few days in London again, this time at
the Angel behind St Clement's Church in the Strand.
Poor Nancy was 'very ill all day and vomitted much and
often', though she recovered sufficiently to do some more
shopping at Charlesworth's in Covent Garden and at a
very good linen-draper's shop kept by a Mr Jeremy, 'a
very civil Man'. She bought 'some Table-Linen, Muslin,
a piece of Holland, Cravats etc.', which amounted to the
extravagant sum of £13 6s., and perhaps it was a good
thing for her uncle's purse that they were leaving for
Norwich the same evening. This time they took the
'Expedition Coach' from the Bull in Bishopsgate,
leaving at nine o'clock and travelling on a very pleasant,
warm moonlit night. But when they got to Newmarket
for breakfast, Nancy discovered that her small red trunk,
'in which were all her principal Matters', had been left
behind in London. She was quite ill with vexation and
Woodforde himself, though he begged her not to worry,
made a great fuss, refusing to pay the second half of their
fare until the trunk was recovered. It was not a very
happy home-coming.

   Once in 1789 and twice more—in 1793 and 1795—they
journeyed down to Somerset and back, though travelling
was then becoming much more expensive. England,
engaged in her desperate struggle with the revolutionary

forces of France, suffered a bad harvest in 1794 and this, combined with the blockade round her coasts, sent the price of corn rocketting up. Gentlemen were urged to give up using flour for powdering their hair, but the cost of a loaf of bread continued to rise alarmingly. The money-lenders grew rich and the poor, already divorced from the land they had worked for hundreds of years by the Enclosure Acts of the previous generation, became still more impoverished. New taxes to pay for the war were levied on almost everything, and while the mail-coaches continued to be subsidized by the Government, a new levy was imposed on the stage-coaches of a half-penny a mile on top of the licence they already had to pay of £5 per annum.

Coach proprietors, protesting vigorously against such unfair competition, had no option but to pass their extra costs on to the public by charging higher fares. Thus the inside fare from Norwich to London, which cost 18s. in 1782, went up to £1 5s. in 1795 and the fare from London to Bath was £1 11s. 6d. instead of £1 1s. Yet there was no falling off in the number of travellers crowding into the coaches. 'We had a very fat Woman with a Dog and many bandboxes, which much incommoded us, and also a poor sickly kind of Man that went with us,' wrote Parson Woodforde of his journey to Bath in 1793, and of the coach from Norwich to London two years later: 'We had four inside Passengers besides ourselves: one very stout Man of Norwich by name Hix, a Grocer, one Single Lady, and a comical Woman with a little Boy her Son, who was sick most part of the night as was the single Woman.'

Prices at the inns along the road were also going up and Woodforde must have had a terrible shock when he added up his accounts for one of his trips into Somerset and back to a total of £78 19s. 7d. Admittedly this staggering figure included two visits to Bath staying at

the White Hart run by Moses Pickwick and his wife, one
of the most expensive and high-class inns in the country,
and several of Nancy's shopping expeditions to the
fashionable Milsom Street, as well as presents for all the
Somerset relations and tips to the servants ministering
to their needs on the road; but 1795 was the last long
journey the parson undertook, perhaps as much for the
sake of his pocket as for the declining state of his health.
After that his relations came to visit him instead, though
'my poor dear Sister Pounsett shook like an aspin Leave
going away', she was so frightened of travelling in a
stage-coach.

Nephew Bill, Nancy's nautical brother, who had
nearly missed the Bath coach in 1786 and was often
severely reprimanded by the parson for his extravagance,
made up for his misdemeanour in January 1803, when
his uncle lay dying. He set off in the Taunton coach from
Castle Cary on 5 January at half-past one in the afternoon, got to London the next day at one o'clock and
caught the mail-coach for Norwich the same evening. On
the 7th he arrived in Norwich and reached Weston
Parsonage at four o'clock in the afternoon of the same
day, 'running in that short time a distance of 238 miles
without 1 minute's sleep'. Unhappily the parsonage was
already 'a House of Mourning' and his uncle could no
longer appreciate the young man's astonishing feat of
endurance or the affection that moved him to hasten
all the way from Somerset to Norfolk: the Rev. James
Woodforde's journey in this life was over and his
nephew had arrived too late.

10

TRAVELLING FOR PLEASURE

PARSON WOODFORDE DID not live to see the turn of the tide in England's great fight against her formidable enemy. He was not much affected by the scarcity of food or the stringency of the measures taken to turn Britain into a fighting nation, and it was still possible to travel about in the seventeen-nineties without seeing much evidence of the struggle for survival that was going on.

Never had the country looked more beautiful or the towns more spacious and elegant. Georgian architects had transformed the narrow medieval streets of the market towns into broad thoroughfares, where the houses, the shops and the inns were all of a good design and the town hall or market place served its integral purpose. The cultured aristocracy, learning about the arts on the almost compulsory Grand Tour abroad and with a mania for building and for redesigning their parks and gardens at home, had given a new loveliness to the land they owned. Peacocks paced the lawns of their gracious Palladian homes and deer browsed under the stately

trees in the park. The undulating landscape of pasturelands and meadows, groves of trees and opulent fields of
corn, seen from their windows, melted into the distant
horizon of the still unravished sea-coast. Stables and
farm buildings of local stone or brick dwelt peacefully
beside the great houses. The church, the manor and the
village still belonged together in a single community and,
through this fusion of their interests, the increasingly
refined tastes of the aristocracy spread among the less
privileged sections of the population with a civilizing
influence never equalled or surpassed.

Nature had been tamed, and not yet wilfully destroyed
for the sake of Mammon. Travellers, who in previous
generations had dreaded losing their way in the wide
open country with all its terrors of accident and violence
on the unfenced roads, now took pleasure in their
journeys. The work of the Adam brothers in architecture,
of Kent, Capability Brown, Repton and their followers
in garden design, had created such harmony in the
landscape, it could be enjoyed not only by the lordly
patrons who employed them, but by anyone passing
through the countryside on top of a stage or a mail-coach.
And this new awareness of the beauty of England was
stimulated by the great school of landscape painters
growing up in the last decade of the century, who for the
first time were conscious of the natural scenery they
observed all around them in the swiftly changing light
of the variable English weather. Gainsborough had been
forced to give up his 'strong inclination for Landskip' in
favour of the more financially rewarding fashionable
portrait and Richard Wilson had died in poverty. But
with Paul Sandby's topographical drawings, Girtin and
Turner working direct from nature in water-colours, the
Norwich School of Crome and Cotman, and John
Constable, born and bred under the windy skies of
Suffolk, painting began to reveal the splendour and the

subtle changes of the countryside through all the seasons
of the year, in the fullness of the summer and the stark
cold of a winter's day. Collectors and patrons encouraged
this new development in English art—it became the
fashion for them to commission views of their houses and
parks as well as portraits of themselves; and to satisfy the
cultural aspirations of the less wealthy classes, a vast
number of topographical publications appeared in the
form of aquatints and engravings issued by the print-
sellers and booksellers in all the important towns and
cities throughout the kingdom.

To be interested in the country had become a mark of
good breeding. Many travellers of the middling sort now
discovered a new enjoyment in the pleasures of sight-
seeing, and road books became indispensable. They were
not without precedent. As early as 1625 Norden had
published *A Guyde for English Travailers, Shewing in
generall how far one Citie and many Shire-Towns in
England are distant from the other*, and in 1675 Ogilby
brought out his *Britannia*, with a geographical and
historical description of the principal roads in England
and Wales; but Paterson's *British Itinerary* first published in 1771 and Cary's *Survey of the High Roads* went
far beyond the original practical purpose of either of
these seventeenth-century publications.

Paterson, a Captain on the staff of the Quarter-
Master General to the Forces, claimed that he was
'animated with a desire of excelling in his profession and
of executing the duties of his staff employment with a
degree of accuracy and precision necessary for conduct-
ing the movements of an army in such regularity and
good order as is absolutely requisite for the good of the
service', and that to achieve this extensive ambition, he
had made a complete study of all the roads, towns and
even villages of note in the kingdom. Certainly his
British Itinerary, which appeared in several editions, was

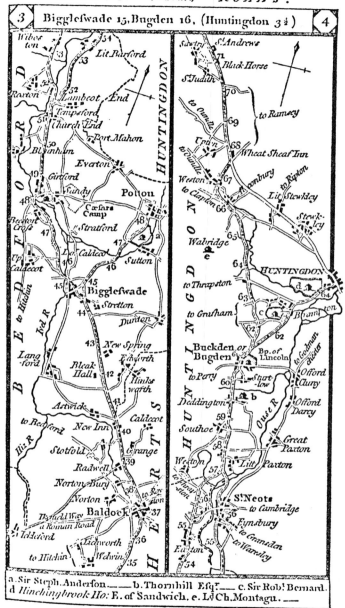

3 Bigglefwade 15, Bugden 16, (Huntingdon 3¼) 4

a. Sir Steph. Anderſon.____ b. Thornhill Eſqʳ.___ c. Sir Robᵗ Bernard.
d *Hinchingbrook Ho:* E. of Sandwich. e. Lᵈ Ch. Montagu. __

Map of the Great North Road from Paterson's British
Itinerary, *1771*   GUILDHALL LIBRARY

a work of quite extraordinary industry, containing maps of all the principal roads and cross-roads in Britain and 'many useful Articles of Information relative to Travelling'. But in 1798 he came into conflict with John Cary, who had started producing a similar work and was in a far stronger position than the Captain, since the Post Office had invited him to make a new survey of all the mail-coach routes and by-roads served by the mail-carts.

Cary received 9d. a mile from the Post Office for his survey and employed a number of men to travel every inch of the roads on foot with a perambulator (which was then nothing to do with a baby-carriage) to record the exact mileage from one point to another. It was natural for him to want to extend his work for publication, even at the risk of infringing Paterson's copyright, and in doing so, he achieved some of the most detailed and fascinating maps ever produced. They were on a scale of one inch to a mile and took notice of 'EVERY GENTLE-MAN'S SEAT, situate on or seen from the ROAD (however distant) with the Name of the Possessor, the Number of INNS on each separate Route and the different Turnpike GATES, shewing the Connection which one Trust has with another'.

In his advertisement to the first edition which had been 'solicited by many Gentlemen', Cary expressed the hope that his work would 'convey to the traveller that kind of information which will give pleasure to his peregrinations, by answering all his enquiries relating to the numberless villas within sight of the road, which so often attract his attention'—and with this purpose in mind, he pinpointed the precise situation of each house, with the name of its owner, by a line drawn to the stretch of road giving the best view of it. Thus any traveller on the road from London to Hampton Court and beyond could not possibly confuse Mr Simkin's house at Turnham Green with Lord Heathfield's, or Lady

Paulett's villa at Twickenham with Mr Huddy's or
Colonel Pechell's, unless the coach was going so fast
there was hardly time to be aware of anything. Information about the Turnpike Trusts was also of great value,
as some tickets allowed the traveller to pass through
more than one gate if several belonged to the same Trust,
and with this certain knowledge, the individual traveller
could avoid many an unpleasant altercation with the
toll-keepers. Coach passengers did not have to worry so
much: the mails went through free of charge and on the
stage-coaches the guard paid for the whole coach. They
did, however, sometimes join in the fray, if the guard or
the coachman started arguing with the toll-keeper,
whose unenviable task of collecting money from people
who resented paying, turned him into a somewhat sour
and disgruntled individual.

Cary's careful note of all the inns on the road was
designed 'to enable a party to form a meeting with
certainty' and was often of great service to coach passengers who had to continue their journey from the inn
where the coach dropped them, either by post-chaise or
by appointment with friends in the district who owned a
private carriage. But coach travellers outside London did
not always have to go to the inn from which the coach
started out; they could take a chance on picking it up
somewhere on the road, or, if they had booked their
places the day before, at some specified point on the
route. The Rev. William MacRitchie, a Scottish minister,
who made an extensive tour of England in the summer
of 1795, came down from Perthshire on horseback as far
as Sharrow, left his horse there with a friend, and at
half-past three in the morning, with a boy carrying his
saddle-bags, set out for the turnpike separating the
counties of York and Derby to take up the seat he had
already booked on the London coach.

As far as Mansfield in Nottinghamshire, his journey

was enlivened by a blind man, called Stevens, who sang like a nightingale and played the fife and the fiddle, much to everyone's delight. The weather was warm and gentle, and MacRitchie, who had never travelled very far outside his native parish of Clunie, enjoyed a wonderful view of the country from the top of the coach. Nottingham, where the coach dined, impressed him greatly: 'the streets, houses and market-place here broad, cleanly and elegant'; and looking back over the Trent after leaving the town, he saw what he believed to be one of the most charming prospects in England. Loughborough he thought was far less attractive, but Leicester another very spacious and beautiful town, and the coach stopped here at six in the evening for tea. Two ladies from Mansfield, two young boys, the sons of a gentleman of fortune living in the neighbourhood of Nottingham, with their French tutor, M. Egrace, and Mr Coleman, a seafaring gentleman from Leicester, made up the rest of the company travelling to London, and they all got on very well together, which was rather surprising, considering MacRitchie was a Presbyterian whose country was at war with France and the boys' tutor a Roman Catholic priest from the other side of the Channel.

They did not have much time to rest. After Leicester they went on to Harborough and thence by starlight to Northampton, arriving there at three o'clock in the morning and leaving almost at once for Newport Pagnell, where they had breakfast. A fine view of the Duke of Bedford's noble house and park at Woburn excited them all and then they came into Hertfordshire, where there were 'hay-makers on every hand and a fine crop appearing everywhere'. In spite of a dreadful thunderstorm, MacRitchie took the outside of the coach again to view the country and was so carried away by his first glimpse of the City from the top of Highgate Hill, he burst into a song of praise. 'Heav'ns! What a goodly

prospect spreads around!' he exclaimed—and indeed it
was, with Wren's great dome of St Paul's dominating the
skyline and all the slender spires of his city churches a
foil to its magnificence.

From the green hills of Highgate and Hampstead,
MacRitchie could see the silver streams of sweet water
winding among the willow trees down the valley into the
Thames, the villages of Islington and St Pancras and
the haymakers in the fields that still stretched out
towards Clerkenwell and Bloomsbury. Even a closer
view of the City did not disillusion him. He spent three
weeks there, visiting all the sights—the Tower and the
Bank of England, Vauxhall Gardens and Westminster—
and when his time was up and he set foot on board the
Cambridge coach on the first stage of his journey home,
he looked back 'with an indescribable mixture of feelings
on this vast Metropolis, well termed "a world of wonders
in itself" '.

It was now the month of August and very hot—too
hot for this young northerner accustomed to the climate
of Scotland: he was in a constant state of perspiration.
Haymaking was still going on, some fields of wheat were
almost ready and some of rye cut down. Near Hoddesdon,
seventeen miles from London, he heard there had been a
great outcry among the people for want of bread,
otherwise he did not apparently see or hear any evidence
of the distress among the poor caused by the war. Being
something of a botanist, he was more interested in
observing from the top of the coach 'some rare plants by
the way-side betwixt Barkway and Cambridge, such as
the *Campanula glomerata, Campanula patula*, and
Asperula Cynanchica', commenting afterwards that
'these stage-coaches are a bad business for botanists'
because, of course, he could not stop and examine the
Campanula more closely.

The country from Cambridge to Huntingdon was

beautiful with lovely willow trees and more wild flowers growing by the side of the road, and at Stamford, where he dined in a great company of travellers, he met a young lady from Ireland, whom he described as 'a character'. Burghley House, belonging to the Earl of Exeter, was now open to the public one day a week and MacRitchie took the opportunity of going round it. He admired the Italian paintings and the splendour of the rooms and the huge trees in the park, 'disposed in the most beautiful and tasty manner', and he was very interested in the Spanish sheep with 'long white tails, bodies speckled black and blue and horns somewhat resembling those of goats'. Burghley was 'justly esteemed one of the finest seats in England' and the chance of seeing it could not be missed, though it meant spending the night at Stamford and when both the mail-coaches came in full early the next morning, waiting for the heavy coach which carried six inside passengers and six outside. Even this was full with only one lady, a clergyman's wife, to eleven gentlemen, one of whom was luckily her husband, and another a Swiss gentleman in England for the first time. With a friendliness that was still rather unusual among the inside and the outside passengers, they all sat down together to dinner at Grantham and enjoyed 'hearty entertainment'.

All the way north from Grantham, MacRitchie saw extensive, well-cultivated farms with 'the corn waving ripe for harvest' and he got out his road book to take note of the gentlemen's seats which could be observed from the top of the coach. Beyond Doncaster, where again he broke his journey to do some sightseeing in the town, he counted no less than seven superb properties, including Squire Finch's Castle and Earl Fitzwilliam's vast estate at Wentworth, but he was very pleased when he got back to Sharrow to find his own horse waiting for him. Much as he had enjoyed his tour, he could now go at his own

9

pace and do any amount of botanizing on his way back to Scotland.

Some travellers among the gentry still preferred riding to any other means of getting about the country. The Hon. John Byng hated going anywhere by coach and never did so if he could avoid it. He took his servant along with him and his own sheets, 'knowing that next to a certainty, 5 sheets must be dirty and 3 damp out of number 10' at most of the inns along the road, while his nightcap, with some other necessities, always travelled behind his own person, in and upon a small cloak bag. 'Walking or riding on a tolerable horse are delights to me,' he declared, 'but box'd up in a stinking coach, dependent on the hours and guidance of others, submitting to miserable associates and obliged to hear their nonsense, is great wretchedness!' Fortunately for this fastidious gentleman, he found 'the vulgarity of women at all times better than the brutality of men', though with five of them in the coach to Leicester—one fat creature like a cook, one large and younger in a linen great coat, another, older, in a blue great coat, and two pert misses from Islington, who talked incessantly of the fashions they had seen at Bagnigge Wells and 'of feathers, robes, bodies and French backs etc.'—he could only sulk along in much heat and inconvenience, so 'bodkined and surrounded by high and wide flat caps' that he could neither stir nor breathe, let alone see out of the window and was 'as much concealed by my guards as could be the Grand-Signor by his Janizaries' Turbans'.

Foreign travellers in England were not too sure about trusting themselves to the public coach either. For one thing, like Byng, they still considered it was beneath their dignity to mix with *hoi polloi* and for another, they found the language problem exceedingly difficult. Very few Englishmen, unless they belonged to the upper classes, ever thought of trying to speak any language

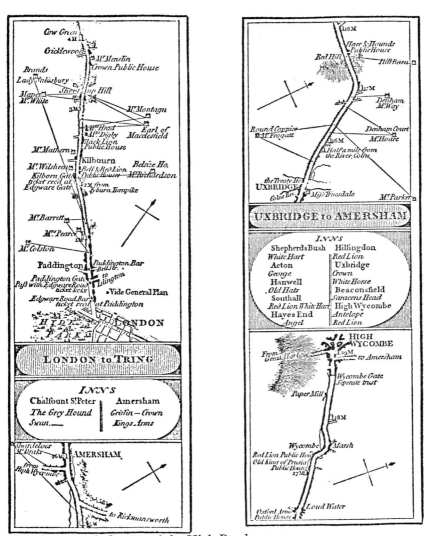

Map from Cary's Survey of the High Roads, *1799*

except their own and the local dialects were so strong, a foreigner with some slight knowledge of English found himself utterly bewildered by the obscure sounds he heard coming from the country people he met on his travels. Louis Simond was in a far stronger position than most. A brilliant and cultured Frenchman, he lived in England from 1810 to 1811 and had married an English wife. He spoke English fluently and in his *Journal of a Tour and Residence in Great Britain* left a lively account of the two short trips he made by coach when he could find no other form of transport between Richmond, where he was staying, and London.

'This morning,' he wrote, 'I set out by myself for *town*, as London is called *par excellence*, in the stage coach, crammed inside and *hérissé* outside with passengers of all sexes, ages and conditions. We stopped more than 20 times on the road—the debates about the fare of the way-passengers—the settling themselves—the getting up, and the getting down, and damsels showing their legs in the operation, and tearing and muddying their petticoats—complaining and swearing—took an immense time. I never saw anything so ill managed.' But this was nothing to the embarrassment of his journey back to Richmond the same evening. 'We found in Piccadilly, a stage coach ready to start for Bath, by which I could be carried some miles on my way,' he reported. 'It resembled a ship on 4 wheels, a sort of half-cylinder, round below, flat above, very long and divided into 3 distinct apartments. I was introduced into the cabin by the after-port, and locked in with another passenger. Soon after I had taken my seat, the carriage rattled away full speed. This was much better than my morning conveyance, and I enjoyed the change; but after a few miles, an apprehension seized me of being carried beyond the part to which I was bound (Kew Bridge). We reached it—I knew it again—saw with terror that we passed it, and that I was

swept away with alarming velocity like Robinson
Crusoe from his island. I endeavoured in vain to call, or
to open the door. At last the carriage stopped unexpectedly, little more than a quarter of a mile beyond the
bridge and proceeding the rest of the way on foot, I
reached Richmond long after dark but in time for
dinner.'

Simond was lucky to be able to get out where he did,
before being overcome with claustrophobia. The freakish
design of the coach he had taken was by no means unusual. Coach-proprietors and coach-builders, faced with
the competition of the mails, were always trying to think
of new ways to attract the public. There was a 'Land
Frigate' to Portsmouth, 'elegantly sashed all round',
which carried no outside passengers in order to preserve
the gentility and respectability of the vehicle, and there
were the 'Light Post Coaches', more expensive and
exclusive than the ordinary stage-coaches. Many of these,
like the one Parson Woodforde took to Bath, were called
'Balloon' coaches, in honour of the first balloon ascent
made by Lunardi in 1784, it being necessary as time went
on and more and more coaches were put on the road to
discover new and attractive names for them that would
distinguish one from the other and describe the character
of the vehicle. Any number of 'Highflyers' appeared on
the Great North Road, designed to appeal to travellers
who put speed before safety, and they were challenged
by the 'Spitfires' and the 'Lightnings', the 'Defiances'
and the 'Telegraph' coaches, which appeared soon after
the system of semaphoring messages between London
and the coast was adopted as a war-time innovation and
the quickest method of communication yet known.

As the long-drawn-out war with France began to turn
in England's favour, coaches were named after Lord
Nelson, the Battle of Trafalgar and the other great
victories achieved by British arms against the aggression

of Napoleon. But England was changing even faster than her coaches were travelling and without her people being really aware of what was happening. While the great aristocratic landowners continued to enjoy the fullness of life and to increase the productivity of their estates by improved agricultural methods, the engrossment of farms and enclosure of the commons deprived the rural peasantry of their long-established rights and reduced them to near starvation at the same time as their cottage industries began to fail in competition with the raw manufacturing towns springing up near the coalfields of the North and the Midlands. The drift to the towns, already noticed by Arthur Young, was accelerated, and the new manufacturers, men of a hard-headed and forceful character intent on thrusting forward to win a larger share of trade overseas through British enterprise and inventiveness, took no thought for the unfortunate men, women and children they put to work their diabolical new machines. Hence the most tragic paradox in history. For at the precise moment when Britain was fighting for the freedom of her people to live as they chose and to destroy the tyranny of a merciless dictator on the Continent, she failed entirely to recognize that she was darkening the lives of more than a third of her population with a new tyranny of her own making. For hundreds of people their old way of life was shattered. Driven from their cottage homes to work in the cotton mills and coalfields, they were herded like cattle into hideous rows of narrow, airless hovels with no sanitation or convenience and an ugliness that damaged their native human dignity for ever. The old harmony of town and country, squire and village, of the farmer and his labourers who sat down together to a wholesome dinner of home-grown food, was disrupted. The Industrial Revolution had begun and in time was to make Britain the most powerful and wealthy nation in the world—at the cost of the most appalling misery a large section of her people had ever known.

It needed a sensitive observer from the New World to realize the full horror of what was going on. Joseph Ballard, a young American from Boston, came to England in the year of Waterloo, and his first sight of Warrington on a Saturday night shocked him beyond belief. He saw men fighting drunk outside the taverns 'in a scene of riot', old women, dressed in filthy rags like the witches in *Macbeth*, driving jackasses delivering coal, and hordes of children swarming in the streets 'in a state of nudity and uncleanliness that was quite disgusting'. Earlier, on leaving Liverpool, he had been amused by the activity of the tumbling boys who turned head over heels at the side of the coach, 'with such swiftness as even to keep up with it some time . . . in expectation that the passengers will throw them a penny', but when he realized their parents were so miserably poor that this was resorted to as a means of subsistence, he was horrified.

All through the manufacturing towns the sight of the children haunted him: 'deprived of education and buried in these dark, noisy, unwholesome dens at the age of eight or nine; besmeared with dirt and grease in the cloth factories in Leeds, where they either pass a quick but miserable existence or furnish turbulent, ignorant and vicious members of society'. And even worse was the attitude of their employers, for when young Ballard, with a good deal of courage, ventured to tackle one of them on the subject, it was only to find him entirely indifferent to their plight. If some children died of exhaustion and malnutrition, or lived to grow into mutilated human beings with no thought in their heads but to drink themselves into a stupor of forgetfulness, there were plenty of others to chain to the buckets of coal and the roaring looms that fed the pockets of the new manufacturers.

Yet it was still only in the North and the Midlands that this ugly new rash was appearing on the gentle face of England. When he left Sheffield on the coach for London, Ballard was soon passing through many fine towns and noticing the beauty of the countryside, the rich cultivation of the fields and the plump cattle grazing in the meadows. He had '3 buxom damsels' in the coach with him and, after travelling through the night, one of them pulled a small bottle of rum out of her 'indispensable' and most kindly asked Ballard 'to partake with her and her companions'. He knew something about horses and coaching. His father had a livery stable in Boston and was responsible for putting the first hackney carriage on the road there; and although Joseph had become an apprentice and finally the partner of an English merchant by the name of Standfast Smith, living in Boston and dealing in carpets, cutlery and other household goods, the technical knowledge he had learnt from his father gave him an added interest in his journey, as well as making him feel a little uneasy. He thought it was quite amazing that a coach fully loaded with passengers and luggage, added to the weight of the vehicle itself, which could not have been less than two tons, should be able to travel at a rate of seven or eight miles an hour; and since by 1815 there was 'not the least derogation from respectability in riding outside', he much preferred it in fine weather, though he realized it was more dangerous in the event of any accident happening and tried to console himself that 'being very strong, the coaches were in some degree guarded'.

He found London rather disappointing and very bewildering and when he left it a month later on the coach for Leeds, he was glad of the pure air, having breathed nothing but coal smoke for so long a time. Like MacRitchie, he travelled north by way of Stamford and Newark and was impressed by the many houses of the

nobility he passed along the road, and he found his
fellow travellers—a gentleman and his lady and another
young lady—very agreeable companions. 'During the
journey,' he wrote, 'I was frequently regaled with
refreshments, which the gentleman had brought and was
so polite as to offer me.' But the unself-conscious
behaviour of the young lady filled him with astonishment. 'We travelled all night,' he continued, 'and at
dusk I was not a little surprised at beholding my fair
fellow traveller, who was quite a pretty girl, take off her
bonnet, tie on her night cap, and leisurely compose
herself to sleep in one corner of the coach, where she
made quite an interesting appearance.' Poor Ballard
envied her coolness—he was much too nervous to settle
down to a quiet nap. 'After going with almost incredible
swiftness,' he concluded, 'we arrived at Leeds at 6
o'clock in the morning, being at the rate of 8 miles and
¼ each hour, including stoppages—a velocity with which
I never desire to travel again.'

11

COLERIDGE, KEATS & MARY WORDSWORTH

OTHER PASSENGERS BESIDES Joseph Ballard often found the speed of coaching too hectic. Coleridge arrived at Hatchett's Hotel in Piccadilly on the morning of 23 November 1807 after travelling all night on the Bristol mail, so 'coach-fevered, coach-crazed and coach-stunn'd', he had to spend the greater part of the day in bed to recover. Yet he admitted that he had dozed away the whole night 'in that sort of *whether-you-will-or-no* slumber' brought on by the easy motion of the vehicle, and even when he had a cold or his stomach was upset, he preferred travelling outside to being cramped up inside.

He went down to Bristol again at the end of the month and returned to London on 2 December, describing his journey at length in a letter to his friends, the Morgans. 'I am arrived in safety,' he wrote, 'but the Coach being quite full, all lusty men but one, and he together with one of the lusty travellers having great Coats on, or rather *huge* Coats that ought at least to have payed half-price, I was terribly cramped, my shoulders in a pillory and my legs in the stocks—in consequence of which my

feet and legs are more swoln than I ever remember them
to have been on a similar occasion. The slenderest of our
company,' he went on, 'was a rather well featured young
Frenchman as I conjectured by his accent and sallow
complexion; who had a livery Servant on the outside and
who seemed intent on acting the part of a young English
Blood or Jockey—now riding outside, now inside—
always going from one to the other by the Coach door on
the wheels—and while in the Coach, eternally pulling up
and down, and making a noise with the window—a more
restless monkey never played Gambols off and on the
perch he was tied to.'

This irritating young man was, however, more acceptable than some of Coleridge's companions on his next
trip from Bristol, when he had a most unpleasant journey
owing to a succession of vicious horses. 'The moonlight,
tho' not always of the clearest, lessened the danger,
which in a dark night would have been very serious'; but
the coach was an hour late arriving and he found his
fellow travellers very uncongenial. They included a
Colonel Peacock, the brother of the Barrack Master at
Malta, 'not held there in high honour for countenancing
General Villette's Intimacies with his wife, Lady Dallan's
Daughter—this Col, a free and easy proud Fool, very
remarkably stupid and uninformed; and a Gentleman or
Merchant, whose jokes and general conversation made it
charitable toward human Nature to hope that his mother
had born and reared him in a Brothel'. Both these
passengers wore enormous great coats which added
considerably to the amount of space they took up, so that
Coleridge was again very annoyed and suffered a great
confinement of his limbs, which made him feel very
unwell.

Yet he was not in the least shy of wrapping himself up
whenever he went on a journey—without apparently
taking into account the inconvenience he may have

caused anyone else sitting on the coach with him. After travelling outside at Christmas-time a few years earlier from London to Bath on his way to Nether Stowey, he wrote: 'I left London on Saturday Morning at 4 o'clock and for 3 hours was in such a storm as I was never before out in; for I was a top of the Coach—Rain and Hail and violent wind with vivid flashes of Lightning, that seemed almost to alternate with flash-like Re-emersions of the waning Moon, from the ever shattered, ever closing Clouds. However I was armed cap-a-pie, in a compleat Panoply, namely, in a huge, most huge Roquelaire, which had cost the Government 7 guineas—and was provided for the Emigrants in the Quiberon Expedition, one of whom falling, stayed behind and parted with his Cloak to Mr Howel who lent it to me. I dipped my head down, shoved it up, and it proved a compleat Tent to me. I was as dry as if I had been sitting by the fire.'

Any journey that meant a change of scene, for a time stimulated Coleridge in his restless search for the health and happiness which never quite came within his reach and began to diminish steadily as the fatal habit of taking opium grew upon him. Sometimes he reacted quite cheerfully to the hazards of the weather and enjoyed himself; at other times he complained bitterly of the damp and the cold and of feeling very ill when he arrived at his destination, and although it was part of his nature to exaggerate his discomforts, he must have suffered a great deal as the coach ran on through the night at speed to keep up with its schedule.

The weather affected Keats also, and travelling in the cold and the damp was the worst thing he could have done. But when he first went to the Isle of Wight on the Southampton coach in 1817, he was unaware of his incipient disease, and although he confessed to feeling 'rather muzzy' after travelling all night, he sent his brothers a gay account of his journey. 'I am safe at

Southampton,' he wrote, 'after having ridden three stages outside and the rest in for it began to be very cold. I did not know the Names of any of the Towns I passed through all I can tell you is that sometimes I saw dusty Hedges sometimes Ponds—then nothing—then a little Wood with trees look you like Launce's Sister "as white as a Lilly and as small as a Wand"—then came houses which died away into a few straggling Barns then came hedge trees aforesaid again. As the Lamp light crept along the following things were discovered: "long heath brown furze"—Hurdles here and there half a Mile—Park palings when the Windows of a House were always discovered by reflection—One Nymph of Fountain *N. B. Stone*—lopped Trees—Cow ruminating—ditto Donkey—Man and Woman going gingerly along—William seeing his Sisters over the Heath—John waiting with a Lanthen for his Mistress—Barbers Pole—Doctor's Shop— However after having had my fill of these I popped my Head out just as it began to Dawn.'

Two years later, when he again went down to the Isle of Wight on the Portsmouth coach, the brightness of the dawn had faded. Keats had watched his brother Tom die of consumption, his poetry had been violently attacked by the critics and his love for Fanny Brawne had become more of a torment than a joy. Travelling on the outside of the coach in a heavy shower, he caught what he dismissed as 'a little cold' in a letter to his young sister, Fanny, entertaining her instead with an account of his fellow travellers. 'There were on the Coach with me,' he told her, 'some common french people, but very well behaved. There was a woman amongst them to whom the poor Men in ragged coats were more gallant than ever I saw gentleman to Lady at a Ball. When we got down to walk up hill—one of them pick'd a rose, and on remounting gave it to the woman with "Ma'mselle—voila une bell rose!" '

The gay Frenchmen left the coach at Portsmouth but the little cold Keats had caught persisted all through the summer and the autumn, with 'a haunting sore throat', and by February 1820, when he started spitting blood, he realized that his illness was mortal. Thereafter the slightest exertion or excitement, whether mental or physical, weakened his resistance, and when he was finally persuaded to sail for Italy to avoid another English winter, his last journey in a hired coach to Gravesend was a nightmare of pain and anguish.

Only the hardiest of travellers could endure the rigours of riding outside on a coach through the night without suffering intensely from the cold. In March 1812 a Wiltshire newspaper reported that on the arrival of the Bath coach at Chippenham, it was found that two of the passengers had frozen to death and a third was dying; and Jane Austen's two brothers, Edward and George, might have suffered a similar fate on their journey down to Southampton four years earlier, if the kind old coachman, Mr Weeks, had not shared the voluminous skirts of his great coat with them when they had foolishly forgotten to provide themselves with sufficient covering. Even so, they arrived stiff with cold and Jane was very anxious about them; thinking they would be in bed next day, she was 'heartily glad' to discover how wrong she was, when instead of suffering from their adventure, they appeared to be very well and to have thrived on the cold night air.

Jane herself, as far back as 1796, had always longed to travel in a stage-coach and was not allowed to. Her brother Frank did not think it was quite nice for a young girl of twenty-one to go anywhere in a public vehicle. When she went to Rowling in Kent to stay with him, he came to fetch her, and when she went to Bath, it was by the more genteel method of travelling by post-chaise and picnicking on the way. Not until she was nearly forty and had already written four of her famous novels, did she get her own way about travelling on the public coach —and then it was in one of the slower stages, called 'Yalden', from Chawton to London. 'I had a very good Journey,' she wrote to her sister, Cassandra, 'not crouded, two of the three taken up at Bentley being Children, the others of a reasonable size; and they were all very quiet and civil. We were late in London, from being a great Load and from changing coaches at Farnham, it was nearly 4 I believe when we reached Sloane St.; Henry himself [another brother] met me, and as soon as my Trunk and Basket could be routed out from all the other Trunks and Baskets in the world, we were on our way to Hans Place in the luxury of a nice large cool dirty Hackney Coach. There were 4 in the kitchen part of Yalden and I was told 15 at top, among them Percy Benn; we met in the same room at Egham, but poor Percy was not in his usual spirits. He would be more chatty I daresay from Woolwich. We took up a young Gibson at Holybourn; and in short either everybody *did* come up by Yalden yesterday or wanted to come up.'

Jane admitted to feeling a little tired after her 'long jumble'. She was not young enough or giddy enough to risk riding on the roof, but with her even temperament and her remarkable good sense, she had no fear of travelling and in this she was extremely fortunate. For many women the fear of going on a journey was as bad, if not worse, than the journey itself and the cause of the sickness that assailed them; they were so frightened of being sick, they succumbed immediately. Poor Sara Hutchinson, the sister-in-law of Wordsworth and the woman Coleridge loved, was constantly embarrassed and in despair at her inability to take a journey without being ill on the way. She had an absolute horror of travelling by coach, yet being single and a tower of

strength in a large family, she was ever in demand as the
kindly and indefatigable support of all her relations.
When illness struck them down or another baby was
expected, they sent for Sara—and she went at once,
without any thought of excusing herself, bravely
enduring the miseries of whatever journey was required
of her: to brother John at Stockton or brother Thomas
and his wife in Wales, to her Monkhouse cousins in
London or at Stow, to Coleridge in Highgate when he was
ill, and back and forth to Westmorland, where she lived
on and off for thirty years with the Wordsworths. On one
of her journeys into Wales with a friend called Mrs
Ellwood, there was 'a drunken young man in the coach,
something like a horse dealer, who smelt of liquor and
slept all the way, tossing about his legs and arms to our
great disgust'—both ladies being so upset by his
behaviour, they left the coach at Ross and continued
their journey to Hereford and beyond by post-chaise,
their tranquility somewhat restored by the superb view
they had of the Welsh mountains in the transparent
light of the evening, but poor Sara feeling very sick and
unable to eat anything at all.

The Wordsworths could not really do without her—
from the day of the wedding reception when William's
sister, Dorothy, lay prostrate on the bed upstairs,
through the birth and bringing up of all their children.
She transcribed William's poems for him when his eyes
were giving him trouble, and he sometimes allowed her
to criticize them. He was extremely fond of her. 'I love
you most tenderly,' he once wrote in a letter begging her
to return quickly from a visit to her brother at Stockton,
and his wife, Mary, added a postcript saying: 'I want you
my most dear sister painfully.' Without Sara the lake-
side household was incomplete.

Mary was thin and overworked in the first years of her
marriage, worn down by the cares of motherhood and

grief at the loss of two of her young children within six months of each other; none the less she was secure in her husband's love and often accompanied him on his journeys to London and elsewhere, leaving her household in the capable hands of Sara. Unlike her sister, she did not suffer from coach sickness and had no fear of travelling, but on one of her trips to London with William in 1816, she lost all her luggage. 'For myself,' she wrote from their lodgings in Cavendish Square, 'I am quite a prisoner not having Pellise, Shawl, Cloak or one earthly thing to go out in, owing to the carelessness of one of the Guards who lost us the most important of our packages, inasmuch as it contained all our needments by the way, and upon our arrival, till such time as we Rustics could put ourselves in proper trim. This being Sunday nothing can be done to-day. We arrived yesterday afternoon and put ourselves into the first empty lodgings we met with, that we found with some difficulty, having lost addresses (in the unfortunate Portmanteau) that would have saved us much trouble.'

Two years later, returning home from another visit to London, a far more curious experience than losing their luggage disturbed them. 'Judge of our dismay,' Mary exclaimed, 'when, having taken our seats at a ¼ before 7 in the morning at Manchester, the Coach pulled up at the House of Correction and took upon its roof no less than 10 convicts with their attendants—we could scarcely see them as they approached, clanking their chains, attended by a concourse of Friends and Wives and Children. They were not speedily arranged, being fastened by threes and fours together. They were going to Lancaster Castle—some for imprisonment, some for temporary transportation and one, I believe, to be transported for life—all equally grey and indifferent to the future.

'It saddened that day's journey,' Mary added—as

10

indeed it must have, if it did not scare the passengers by
reminding them too closely of the shocking state of the
nation. For the England that emerged victorious from
the Battle of Waterloo suffered in the first five years of
peace a sharp decline in trade and one crisis after another
in agriculture. Her people, almost as soon as they had
finished rejoicing over the final and utter defeat of
Napoleon, suddenly discovered the dislocation and the
cost of a war that had lasted on and off for twenty years.
The price of corn dropped from 120s. a quarter in 1813
to 53s. 6d. in 1816; hundreds of farmers were ruined, and
the poor, who had been driven to earn their living in the
manufacturing towns, could not afford a loaf of bread. A
slump in world trade caused thousands of men, women
and children to be laid off by their new masters without a
penny in their pockets, and the return of the soldiers and
sailors, discharged without so much as one shilling in
compensation for their service to the nation, made a
situation, already menacing, explosive.

Not since the Civil War had the common people been
so bewildered by the sudden and terrible distress that
came upon them and never had they felt so much
bitterness. Cut off from the land in squalid towns,
dominated by the noisy, smoky factories that had served
the nation in the war and now were idle, there was
nothing they could do within the law to express their
fury and their anguish. Riots and demonstrations were
treated with the utmost severity and the penalty for
poaching game was raised to transportation for seven
years or the gallows. The rich landowners were afraid
of damage to their property and the manufacturers of
bankruptcy, while the Government, caught by surprise
and without a single constructive idea, ordered the
starving people to be suppressed and the magistrates to
pass heavy sentences on the transgressors. No wonder
Mary Wordsworth thought the victims appeared 'all

equally grey and indifferent to the future'—they had none.

But Mary was a loving and a sensitive woman, moving in a circle of poets who were less blind to the social injustices of these years than most of the men and women of their generation. She brought her children up to be good citizens and encouraged them to develop into balanced human beings, nourishing their independence within the bond of family affection that tied them all together. Considering she had watched two of her family waste away and die of some unspecified disease, she was surprisingly unfussy about her youngest son, Willy. Writing to her cousin, Thomas Monkhouse, to make arrangements for the boy's return to Rydal Mount from Charterhouse, she said: 'We have no fear of trusting him by the Mail—provided you or Mr Johnson [the head-master] give him in charge either to the guard, coachman or any respectable Passenger. People travelling are always kind to Children—and he is a *fendy* lad—only pray impress upon him that he is not to get upon the outside, and above all to avoid leaning over the doors of the Coach. So many accidents have happened to Children from the doors being ill-fastened that this is an idea that rather frightens me. Of course we should be very happy to have him put under Mr Fawcett's care or that of any other Gentleman; but not to wait for it for more than two or three days—because people are apt to put off journeys—and then time is frittered away.'

It was a very long journey for a small boy of eleven to undertake on his own, especially if he had to resist the temptation of leaning out of the window when he got bored with sitting in the coach. He could have travelled via Manchester or Liverpool to Kendal, or in the Glasgow mail to Penrith, a distance of 284 miles, taking two nights and three days of hard going. Either way he would have found plenty of people travelling in the same direction,

for the Lake District and Scotland had by now become
highly popular with tourists from all parts of England.
Mountain scenery no longer inspired people with horror;
it had become romantic and uplifting. James Losh, a
lawyer, describing his journey on the Penrith stage-
coach in 1816, wrote: 'The drive up the Lake of Winan-
dermere in the evening as far as Bowness,—the setting
sun,—the fine moon, etc. filled my mind with a pleasing
tranquillity to which it has for a long time been a
stranger. I trust I shall be a happier and a better man in
consequence of the thoughts and feelings of this evening.'

So many people had, in fact, discovered the Lakes by
1818, that Keats on his walking tour with Brown,
jokingly said: 'Lord Wordsworth instead of being in
retirement, has himself and his house full in the thick
of fashionable visitors quite convenient to be pointed
out all the Summer long.' But Ambleside, a mile and a
half from Rydal, was about as far as the roads were fit
for wheeled traffic to go and travelling to the Lakes, for
anyone unlucky enough to take the wrong coach, could
still be very difficult indeed. Coleridge on his way to
Kendal in 1812, having missed the mail, had taken what
he afterwards learnt was 'deemed the worst Coach on
the road', familiarly known as the 'Lousy Liverpool'.

'I breakfasted at Oxford and stayed more than an
hour,' he wrote to his friends, the Morgans, 'but was
afraid to send for my nephews lest they should be
quizzed by their fellow collegiates, such was the Pothouse
at which the Stage landed, such the ridiculous appearance of the Coach, with 14 distinct gaudy Pictures
painted on it—and we were so followed both in and out
the city by a mob of Boys, shouting out—Lazy Liverpool; Lousy Liverpool—! Here comes long, lazy, lousy
Liverpool—! And truly the Coach deserves it's honours—
Two *such* wretches were forced on me all night, half
drunk, and their Cloathes crusted over with dirt, the

best portion of it from the mud into which they had fallen in a squabble and the worst part filth of their own making.—Two large *ticks*, i.e. Λουσες, I have found on me—and I had taken the precaution to put my bank notes into my breast-plate, but not liking money to lie so near my heart, or to tell the silly truth, not liking it to touch the little remembrancer of affection which I wear there, I therefore put the money into my watch-fob. And sure enough in the night, while dozing, I felt a hand at my small Cloathes—and starting up, the *handy* Gentleman said he was afraid I was cold and so was only putting up the straw round my Legs. Kind Creature! Meantime, the Guard and Coachman (the last especially) had such ferocious phyzzes, that I thought it prudent not to complain to the Proprietors—so on my arrival here [at Birmingham] I quitted the Concern and have taken a place in the Bang-up for Liverpool at 6 o'clock to-morrow morning . . . I itched all over me and was miserable till I could shift myself, and have my hair combed out by a Hair-dresser.'

Fortunately the 'Bang-up', although it was late starting out and two hours late arriving, gave Coleridge a better run to Liverpool and proved to be a clean and respectable coach. One of the passengers, a Mr Adam Wilson, first mate of an East-Indiaman, who had twice been taken prisoner and twice ship-wrecked, was a well-informed, intelligent young man, 'handsome and with agreeable and gentlemanly manners'; but the other passenger, 'a semi-demi-anglicized Dutch German' who worked as a jeweller, was quite the opposite: 'a most presumptuous overflowing and perennial Coxcomb, whose English splash-dashed on in a true torrent, at once vapid and *broken*', making sleep on the journey impossible.

Meanwhile, at the same time as the friends and admirers of Wordsworth and his circle were crowding to the Lake

District, a new interest in Scotland had been roused by *The Lay of the Last Minstrel* and the romantic novels of Sir Walter Scott. Tourists, curious to see the noble surroundings of their favourite author at Abbotsford, made it a place of pilgrimage, and visitors more intimate with Scott lost no opportunity of travelling there to enjoy his princely hospitality. The journey to the North from London had been revolutionized by the mail-coach: in 1786 by the 'Sixty-Hour Coach' to Edinburgh when it first came swinging into the Canongate with the guard blowing his horn, the canon firing from the Castle walls and all the bells of the city ringing out; and in 1788, after much pressure had been brought to bear on the Post Office, by the first Royal Mail direct from London to drive up to the Saracen's Head in Glasgow, where it was drenched in brandy by the excited citizens. Thereafter the two coaches went every day of the week, except Wednesday, running neck and neck to Ferrybridge, where the Edinburgh mail branched off to York and Northallerton and the Glasgow ran parallel to it as far as Scotch Corner, before turning north-west to Greta Bridge, Penrith and Carlisle.

The road from Carlisle to Glasgow was a difficult one to maintain; members of the Glasgow Corporation, the Chamber of Commerce and many of the individual citizens contributed large sums of money to the Turnpike Trust to keep it in repair, rather than suffer the indignity of losing their own direct route to London and having to travel via Edinburgh instead. It crossed the border into Scotland at Gretna Green, where it is said an average of two runaway couples a day arrived, usually at six o'clock in the morning on the mail-coach, to be married before their irate parents could catch up with them. But when Shelley eloped with Harriet Westbrook in August 1811, he chose to carry her off on the Edinburgh mail, after putting his father off the scent by pretending he was going to Holyhead *en route* for Ireland. Nervously trying to convince himself that he was doing a noble act, and with Harriet being sick and miserable for most of the way, their journey was not a very happy one. They passed through York at midnight without having time to call on the poet's friend, Hogg, though Shelley wrote him a letter begging the loan of £10 and managed to give it to someone to deliver by hand. Being disappointed in the expectation of receiving his usual allowance from his father, though he might have known how angry Sir Timothy was, he was desperate for money and had none left by the time they reached Edinburgh; it had not occurred to him that coach fares to Scotland were expensive with any number of extras to be paid for on the way.

Colonel Hawker, who took the Glasgow mail in 1812 with his servant travelling outside, made a more careful calculation of his costs than Shelley. The inside fare amounted to £10 8s. and the outside to £6 10s., and there were tips to six long-stage coachmen at 2s. each— all these paid by Colonel Hawker himself as the inside passenger and the same at half-price for his servant travelling outside. The total amount for the two of them came to £19 10s., and this did not include refreshments and tips to the innkeepers on the way—not that the mails gave anyone very much time to enjoy a hearty meal or to rest for long, unless they stopped somewhere where the business of the Post Office required a longer wait than usual.

Night and day it took no more than two or three minutes to change the horses at each stage along the route and the guards were adept at throwing the mail-bags into the arms of the post-masters without even stopping the coach. Time-keeping was still of the utmost importance as it had been from the very beginning and the mail-coaches were still the most reliable vehicles on

the road. Even in bad weather, in frost and snow and
sleet, the coachmen and the guards took pride in bringing
the coach to its destination on time. But disaster upset
the up mail from Glasgow to London in 1808, when the
bridge at Elvanfoot collapsed and the coach plunged
into the swollen waters of the river. Two passengers
and three horses were drowned, the coachman, the
guard and everyone else being seriously injured, and the
down mail would have met with the same dreadful
accident, if the screams of the hurt passengers fighting
to save themselves, had not warned the coachman just
in time for him to rein up his team on the brink of the
angry torrent.

At first 'the marvellous velocity of nearly 7 miles an
hour' was considered 'highly dangerous to the head,
independent of all the perils of turnover', according to
Lord Campbell, the Lord Chancellor, who often travelled
on the 'Sixty-Hour Coach' from Edinburgh. Men and
women who reached London with such celerity were said
to have 'died suddenly of an affection of the brain', and
Campbell's family and friends were so alarmed for him,
they advised him to stay at least a day in York to
recruit himself. Stories of accidents to the famous
coach were deliberately fabricated by jealous stage-coach
proprietors who could not compete with its speed, and on
one occasion they bribed a number of belligerent carters
to block the road five miles from Haddington; the coachman and the guard were beaten up and badly hurt, but
highly praised by the passengers for the way they dealt
with this unlooked-for incident. And there was no stopping the 'Sixty-Hour Coach' or the number of travellers
who availed themselves of its rapid journey from
London.

Even the Scots themselves with their canny suspicion
of the Sassenachs, learnt to appreciate the punctuality of
the mails, and very soon the system was extended to

connect twenty-two Scottish towns with Edinburgh. In
1740 it had taken Lord Lovat twelve days to creep south
from Beauly near Inverness to the Scottish capital,
where he arrived with his travelling carriage in pieces,
though it had twice been rebuilt on the way. Now it was
possible to dine in Edinburgh one day and to breakfast
at Inverness the next morning, unless the coach was held
up by a blizzard; and in 1819, when the new bridge over
Dornoch Firth was opened, mail-coaches began running
to Thurso in the far north only twenty miles short of
John o'Groats, thus completing the last link in the chain
of fast transport first conceived by John Palmer of Bath.

This astonishing feat could not, however, have been
achieved without the untiring work of another remarkable individual, who gave Scotland some of the finest
roads in the kingdom. Thomas Telford was born in
Eskdalemuir, the son of a shepherd in the lonely hills of
Dumfriesshire, and he might have been content to
follow his father's calling if his extraordinary, precocious
talent for drawing had not attracted the attention of
the local stone-mason, who took him on as an apprentice.
At twenty-four, having completed his apprenticeship, he
set off on foot for Edinburgh with his tools on his back
and sixteen shillings in his pocket. The New Town was
still in the process of being built and stone-masons were
in great demand; but a chance visit to London, where he
was sent as a messenger, altered the whole course of the
young man's future. He went for six days—and stayed
six years, living frugally on his wages, working all day
and studying all night, until he was sufficiently qualified
in mathematics, engineering and architecture to apply
for the post of Roads Surveyor for Shropshire.

His appointment surprised everyone, except himself;
there was no other Road Surveyor quite like him and his
programme was unique. With enormous energy and
persistence, he set about building bridges over the River

Severn, flattening the hills and filling in the valleys to re-align the main highways to meet the needs of the traffic hurrying along them. Opposition from the landed gentry, the Turnpike Trusts and finance committees made no difference to this inspired engineer-architect, whose grasp of the science of road-making had not been equalled since the days of the Romans; and in 1800, when the distressing state of the Scottish Highlands at last induced the Government to take remedial action, Telford was given supreme power over the whole area. In eight years he built mile upon mile of hard road across hitherto impassable bog, mountain and heather, bridged one thousand, one hundred and seventeen rivers and created twenty new ports to serve the fishing industry. Then, at the urgent request of the Government, he was invited south again to reconstruct the London to Holyhead route, which petered out beyond Chester in a quagmire of mud. The former shepherd boy was a genius —and for once the Government showed its nerve in not grudging him the high price of around £1,000 a mile which the new road cost.

Meantime, another persevering Scot had been making his own experiments in road surfacing in Ayrshire. John Loudon MacAdam, born about a year before Telford, was the descendant of an ancient Scottish family. As a young man he went to live with an uncle in America and made a fortune out of selling prize ships in the Revolutionary War, returning to Scotland in the seventeen-nineties to live the life of a landed gentleman. As a trustee for the Ayrshire roads, he found them quite inadequate for the new fast coaches, expensive to repair and, once they were repaired, reduced at once by the amount of traffic they carried to the same state as before. To harden the surface with a thin layer of broken stones, as nearly as possible of the same size, would, he thought, allow the rain to drain away at the same time as the carriage wheels pressed the angular fragments more closely together.

Even Telford had not discovered a permanent surface for his roads, and it was MacAdam's good fortune to be able to test his theories by patiently driving up and down the temporary surface he laid in the grounds of his own estate. Then in the year of Waterloo, when he was sixty, he became Surveyor of the Bristol Roads and was able to give his experiment a further, more gruelling test on the public highway. The whole of the road from Bristol to Bath was 'macadamized' and gave such satisfaction that no one was left in any doubt about its superiority over all other known methods of road surfacing, and MacAdam in due course became Surveyor-General of all the highways in the kingdom. With his innovation and Telford's system of road construction, the Golden Age of coaching had dawned and was soon to become the envy and the wonder of the world.

12

THE
GOLDEN AGE

IT WAS THE success of the mail-coach system that put
the stage-coach proprietors on their mettle. Men of the
new generation, brought up in Regency England and
continuing to prolong its spirit of zest and enjoyment
after the fat and eccentric Prinny had been crowned
King George IV, were no longer content with the pace of
their predecessors. Speed, smartness and efficiency were
the criterion of the age. The days were over when any
kind of vehicle could be put on the road with any kind of
coachman pushing along a team of broken-down cattle;
only thoroughbred horses could stand up to the new
speeds of ten or eleven miles an hour on the macadamized
roads and only the new kind of coachman, a 'swell-
dragsman' of smart appearance and polished manners,
who took pains to understand the art of driving, could
consistently maintain the high level of performance
required by the travelling public and the coach masters.
The smaller undertakers, except on the cross roads of
minor importance, were squeezed out by the three or
four big men operating in each town, whose organization of the whole coaching business of the nation reached
immense proportions in the years between 1820 and 1840.

In London there were four leading competitors: William Chaplin, Edward Sherman, Benjamin Worthy Horne and Robert Nelson; and two ladies: Mrs Ann Nelson of the Bull Inn, Aldgate, and Mrs Ann Mountain of the Saracen's Head, Snow Hill. The two ladies were content with a comparatively small but rich mouthful of the coaching cake. Mrs Mountain, a woman of great vitality, decided to carry on when her husband died in 1818, and with the help of her son, Peter, managed to keep her coach factory behind the Saracen's Head and her coaching business going for a number of years. Thirty of her coaches left from the yard of the Saracen's Head every day of the week, among them the Birmingham 'Tally-Ho!', a fast day coach, which she established in 1823 and maintained against the ruthless competition of the 'Independent Tally-Ho!', put on the same road by William Horne in an attempt to run Mrs Mountain's 'Tally-Ho!' off it. Passengers in either coach needed very stong nerves, since the coachmen raced each other furiously over the whole distance and were bitter enemies, Horne's 'Independent Tally-Ho!' beating all coaching records on May Day 1830 by covering the 109 miles to Birmingham in seven and a half hours at an average speed of fourteen and a half miles per hour.

Mrs Nelson, like Mrs Mountain, was a widow and no less vigorous in the way she conducted her business from the Bull Inn, Aldgate. Being situated on the turnpike leading out of London to the east, she had quite a monopoly of the coach traffic to the eastern counties, as well as running the Exeter 'Defiance', a famous long-distance night coach. She refused to change the name of the Bull Inn to the Bull Hotel when it became more snobbish and more fashionable to use the word hotel, secure in the knowledge that hers was a very good house with every comfort for her guests. Up every morning very early, she kept an energetic, personal eye on everything and was particularly generous in the way she treated her coachmen and her guards, reserving a special room at the Bull for their private use and giving them a free banquet once a year. Her guards, who were experts on the key-bugle, sometimes used on the road instead of a coaching-horn, played a selection of music in the yard at her request to entertain the travellers waiting to go off in one of her coaches or to welcome those arriving tired after a long journey.

All three of Mrs Nelson's sons were in the coaching business. John, the eldest, helped her to run the Bull Inn, George drove the Exeter 'Defiance' and Robert, who inherited his mother's force of character, set up on his own at the Bell Savage, now called La Belle Sauvage, on Ludgate Hill. How the inn where Parson Woodforde had been so badly 'bit by the Buggs' came to be called La Belle Sauvage is not precisely known. Some time in the eighteenth century the landlord adopted the figure of an Indian woman holding a bow and arrow as his sign, and this was identified by Thackeray with 'the sweet American Pocahontas'. Other writers, however, believed the beautiful savage was Princess Geneviève, the heroine of a French romance entitled *La Belle Sauvage*, and still others have connected her with the Queen of Sheba or the Patient Griselda. But whatever the cause of the name being changed from its original form, it was Robert Nelson who brought La Belle Sauvage up to date as a coaching inn and as such it remained until 1850, when John Cassell established his publishing house on the premises.

Robert Nelson took over from Robert Gray, a smaller coach-proprietor, who moved to the Bolt in Tun in Fleet Street, and he soon worked up a considerable business. From five o'clock in the morning until eight or nine, while the day coaches were loading up and going out and the night coaches coming in, the great yard of La Belle Sauvage was in a constant hum of excitement—ostlers

shouting, horses shaking their harness and kicking the
ground, servants running backwards and forwards with
boxes and bundles of baggage and the coachmen and the
guards impatiently fussing to be off. Half-awake passengers, hustled out of their beds before dawn, pulled on
their boots and tumbled down the stairs in the dark to
take their places on the outgoing coaches, with only
enough time for a nip of brandy and hot water. Bleary-
eyed travellers unpacked themselves from the night
coaches, stretched out their aching limbs and hastened
into the well-furnished coffee room for breakfast, which
was, in fact, a feast of cold pigeon-pie, boiled beef and
ham, grilled kidneys and bacon, poached eggs, buttered
toast and muffins—all this washed down with hot tea or
coffee, if not with something stronger, for travelling by
coach induced a hearty appetite and Robert Nelson had
to keep La Belle Sauvage up to standard or fall behind
his competitors.

He kept about four hundred horses in his stables and
ran several fast day and night coaches to Bath, Cheltenham, Brighton, Cambridge and Manchester. The 'Star' to
Cambridge was driven up in the morning and back again
in the afternoon by Jo Walton, a crack coachman,
second to none on the road, who disliked tiresome
female passengers bothering him about their luggage and
their parcels. The 'Red Rover' to Manchester, besides
being painted scarlet, was decked out with red harness
for the horses and red coats for the guard and the coachman, and when Sherman of the Bull and Mouth succeeded in running the 'Red Rover' off the road with a
rival vehicle, Robert Nelson promptly started a new fast
coach called the 'Beehive', 'with superior accommodation
for comfort and safety to any coach in Europe'. Every
luxury had been thought of, for the advertisement went
on to announce: 'The inside of the coach is fitted up with
spring cushions and a reading-lamp, lighted with wax,

for the accommodation of those who wish to amuse themselves on the road. The inside backs and seats are also fitted up with hair cushions rendering them more comfortable to passengers than anything hitherto brought out in the annals of coaching, and, to prevent frequent disputes respecting seats, every seat is numbered. Persons booking themselves at the coach office will receive a card, with a number upon it, thereby doing away with the disagreeables that occur daily in the old style.' Moreover, to insure safety and punctuality with respectability, it was stated that 'no large packages will be taken, or fish of any description carried by this conveyance'.

No fish and a reading-lamp were something even Sherman and Chaplin, the two biggest coach-proprietors of all, never seem to have thought of in considering the comfort of their passengers. Edward Sherman was probably too keen on making a fortune to bother very much about fish of any description, unless he could see a profit in carrying parcels of it from the coast to London. The comfort of his passengers did not bother him very much, either, so long as they did not take their custom elsewhere and patronize one of his rivals' vehicles. He was hard-headed and utterly ruthless in his methods. Unlike most of the big proprietors, he could not drive a coach and knew very little about horses, having started life as a stockbroker in association with a Jewish friend, Lewis Levy, who farmed turnpike tolls to the tune of half a million pounds a year and helped to put his ally in the coaching business.

Not to be outdone by Lewis Levy, Sherman had, in the meantime, married three elderly widows in quick succession and, with the money they bequeathed to him, he acquired the old Bull and Mouth in St Martin's-le-Grand, a famous inn, originally called the Boulogne Mouth in honour of Henry VIII's capture of Boulogne Harbour.

SIX O'CLOCK IN THE MORNING
ℑrom London.

Respectfully inform the public and their friends in particular, that, for their more *perfect convenience*, and to keep pace with the daily improvements in travelling, *the hour of its leaving London will be altered* on Monday the 13th of May, (and continued during the summer months,)

TO SIX O'CLOCK IN THE MORNING,
Instead of Night.

The arrangements that are forming in furtherance of this long-desired alteration, will ensure a steady and punctual conveyance of Passengers to Stamford by a Quarter before Six o'clock, and to Melton by a Quarter before Nine o'clock in the Evening.

The hours of leaving Melton and Stamford will NOT be altered.

The proprietors take this opportunity to acknowledge their sense of the decided patronage shown to the REGENT COACH under their several regulations, and to repeat their promise that no exertion shall be wanting to make it one of the most desirable conveyances to and from London.

Passengers and Parcels booked at Mr. Weldon's, and the Bull and Swan Inn, Stamford; and at Mr. Sharpe's, Bell Inn, Melton.—*Stamford, May 1, 1822.*

Drakard.

Speed, smartness and efficiency on the Regent Coach, 1822

MANSELL COLLECTION

The name had long since become anglicized and Sherman was clever enough not to try and change it; instead he adopted the sign depicting a man's head with a bull inside its enormously wide mouth, as his symbol, and had it painted on the door panels of his smart yellow and black coaches. Situated immediately opposite the new General Post Office building in St Martin's-le-Grand, the Bull and Mouth was in a strategic position for the mail-coach business and had been the headquarters of Willans, one of the earliest contractors for horsing the mails out of London. But Sherman was not content with his share of the mail-coach contract. Though it gave great prestige to the coach masters and entitled them to call their premises Royal Mail-Coach Offices, there was not enough money in it to satisfy the ex-stockbroker, and in 1825 he established a more paying proposition when he put the Shrewsbury 'Wonder' on the road, a fast day coach leaving the Bull and Mouth early in the morning and arriving at the Lion in Shrewsbury fifteen hours later.

A stud of one hundred and fifty horses was kept exclusively for the use of this famous coach and people who travelled by it never forgot the excitement it caused, boasting of their journey for the rest of their lives. Sam Hayward, its celebrated coachman on the run from Birmingham to Shrewsbury, used to bring the coach up the steep hill of Wyle Cop at a gallop, turn the horses in their own length and drive them through the archway into the yard of the Lion at a smart trot, with only an inch to spare on either side of the vehicle and all the outside passengers ducking their heads for fear of being scalped. 'I think I'll get off,' one nervous outsider was said to have murmured, only to be told: 'You be damned!' as Hayward performed this astonishing feat with absolute precision and great pride in his own skill. An attempt by Benjamin Worthy Horne to run the 'Wonder' off the road with a coach called the 'Nimrod' failed. Sherman retaliated with another coach, the 'Stag', timed to run ahead of the 'Nimrod', while the 'Wonder' ran just after it, and he deliberately reduced the fares on both of his coaches, so that very few people wanted to patronize the 'Nimrod', and any travellers who did were liable to end up in a state of nervous collapse at the coachman's effort to outdistance the 'Stag' and the 'Wonder'.

Sherman's tough and tight-fisted methods of running his business brought him great prosperity. He rebuilt the Bull and Mouth in 1830, greatly extending the accommodation for the huge number of travellers coming in and going out every day, and he also built underground stables beneath the yard, big enough to hold seven hundred horses. In this he was imitating William Chaplin, whose business was even more extensive and whose knowledge of horses and everything to do with coaching far exceeded that of anyone else in the field.

Chaplin was the son of a coachman with a small business on the Dover Road. Strong and energetic, with a keen perception of the mutability of human nature and a generous heart, he grew up with every instinct tuned to the life of the road, and when he took over the Swan with Two Necks in Lad Lane off Gresham Street, he very soon showed his capacity by the shrewd and honourable way he conducted his affairs. The name of the inn and its sign of a double-necked swan was a popular corruption of the original Swan with Two Nicks, which referred to the custom of the Vintners' Company of marking their young swans on the upper reaches of the Thames with two nicks to distinguish them from the royal swans marked with five. John Palmer's first mail-coach from Bath had driven into its yard when it was owned by Wilson, and it was already well-known to travellers from all parts of Britain as one of the best

houses in London; but it was in Chaplin's time that the
yard drew crowds of spectators every day to watch the
splendid pageant of the spick-and-span coaches setting
out on their long journeys, with the glossy horses
groomed to perfection and their harness shining, and the
coachmen skilfully negotiating the notoriously narrow
gateway into Lad Lane.

Chaplin worked day and night to perfect the running of
his multifarious concerns, keeping the welfare of his
passengers and his staff under his constant personal
supervision, and while few men ever got the better of
him, none ever found him unjust or malicious or failed
to respect his integrity. At one time his elegant red and
black vehicles with the eighteen hundred horses he owned
served no fewer than sixty-eight different routes, and
the people he employed as coachmen, guards, horse-
keepers, ostlers, stable-boys and storekeepers numbered
close on two thousand. Of the twenty-seven mails
leaving London every night, he horsed fourteen on the
first stage in and out of the City and several of them on
the next stage down the road. The Devonport 'Quicksilver', the Holyhead, the Bristol and five other West
Country mails left from Piccadilly, and the passengers
who had booked at the Swan with Two Necks were
carried to the Gloucester Coffee House or the White
Horse Cellar by Chaplin's omnibus.

Lord William Pitt Lennox, a son of the Duke of
Richmond and a great coaching enthusiast, described the
scene in Piccadilly before the coaches got off. 'What a
confusion!' he wrote. 'What a Babel of tongues! People
hurrying hither and thither, some who had come too
soon, others too late. There were carriages, hackney
coaches, vans, carts, and barrows; porters jostling,
touters swearing, cads elbowing, coachmen wrangling,
passengers grumbling, men pushing, women scolding.
Trunks, portmanteaux, hat-boxes, band-boxes, strewed

the pavement; orange merchants, cigar merchants, umbrella merchants, dog merchants, sponge merchants, proclaiming the superiority of their various wares; pocket knives with ten blades, a corkscrew, button-hook, punch, picker, lancet, gimlet, gun screw, and saw; trouser-straps, four pairs a shilling; silver watch-guards —"cheap, very cheap"; patent pens and (n)ever-pointed pencils, twelve a shilling; bandana handkerchieves, that had never seen foreign parts, to be given away for an old hat; London sparrows, as the coachman would say, "yellow bodies", passed off as canaries; ill-shaven curs looking like the priest in the child's story, "all forlorn", painted, powdered, and decked with blue ribbons to assume the form of French poodles who "did everything but speak"; a yard and a half of songs for a half-penny and *Larks in London*, pictorially illustrated, for one shilling . . . The remainder of the group consisting of perambulating piemen, coachmen out of place, country clods, town cads—gaping, talking, wondering; the din occasionally interrupted by a street serenade, the trampling of cattle, or the music of the guard's horn.' With all these distractions, it was surprising that the mails still got off on time. Somehow the passengers sorted themselves and their luggage out and perhaps were grateful for the umbrellas or the pies and the oranges they had been tempted to buy, though whether the sponge vendors had any success is doubtful, and the travellers who bought a dolled-up puppy or a caged bird to take on their journey, cannot have been very popular with their fellow passengers.

Chaplin horsed the West Country mails as far as Hounslow, where he had another large establishment and kept the pick of some of his horses. He was, however, greatly concerned at this time by the falling off in the number of mail-coach travellers, for many people who had previously travelled on the mails now preferred the fast day coaches to travelling all night and arriving at their destination before anyone was properly awake to receive them. Not that this worried young Joseph Paxton, when, at the age of twenty, he was offered the post of head gardener to the Duke of Devonshire. He left London by the coach for Chesterfield and arrived at Chatsworth at a quarter past four in the morning on 9 May 1826. As no one was about, he got over the green-house gates by the old covered way, explored the pleasure grounds and looked round the outside of the house, then went down to the kitchen garden, scaled the wall and saw everything he wanted to see. 'At six o'clock,' he wrote, 'I set the men to work, got Thomas Weldon to play me the waterworks and afterwards went to break-fast with poor dear Mrs Gregory and her niece; the latter fell in love with me and I with her and thus completed my first morning's work at Chatsworth before 9 o'clock.'

Arriving early did not worry the men of mercantile spirit belonging to the North and the Midlands, either—even if their journeys did not always end as happily as Joseph Paxton's. The ever-increasing power of the Industrial Revolution at work in towns like Liverpool, Manchester and Birmingham, put more travellers than ever on the road and, without booking in advance, it was difficult to get a seat on any of the mails or the long-distance day coaches to the busy manufacturing centres. Competition between the proprietors on these favoured routes reached the extremes of open warfare in the twenties and the thirties of the new century. Chaplin owned the Manchester 'Defiance' and the Birmingham 'Greyhound', two of the most reliable fast coaches, but Sherman put the Manchester 'Telegraph' on the same road, which went even faster than the 'Defiance', and both Mrs Mountain and William Horne tried to monopo-lize the road to Birmingham with their 'Tally-Ho!'

coaches. William Horne of the Golden Cross, Charing Cross, dropped down dead at the age of forty-five, worn out by the strain of keeping up the battle, but his son, Benjamin Worthy Horne, who took over the business, was even more ruthless in the methods he used to crush down his competitors. He once brought the coach of one of his enemies to a standstill by driving up to the inn where it normally stopped and buying up all the horses overnight, so that there were none to harness to the coach when it arrived—without a thought, apparently, for the plight of the unfortunate passengers stranded in the middle of their journey.

And, indeed, the public very often got the worst of the bargain in all this cut-throat competition between the coach-proprietors. They had to suffer the fears and the torment of the rival dragsmen racing each other, the inconvenience of being hurried on their feet when they were turned off the coach to walk up a steep hill and the nervous apprehension of some accident occurring owing to the coachman's insane obsession with speed. One of the most terrible accidents happened in 1820, when the Chester mail raced the Holyhead mail and both of the coachmen, Thomas Perdy and George Butler, were charged at Hertford Assizes with the wilful murder of William Hart, who had been thrown off the Holyhead mail and killed instantly. Another of the passengers, Mr Archer, a respectable bootmaker of Cheapside who had his leg and his arm fractured, gave evidence at the trial in a written statement. He was riding on the box beside Perdy on the Holyhead mail on the road out of Highgate, he said, when he saw the Chester mail coming up behind. Both coachmen began to whip their horses and put them into a gallop, driving abreast of each other at high speed for a considerable distance, until Butler, on the Chester mail, was apparently overcome by the impropriety of his conduct and slackened his pace. But

when the coaches were approaching St Albans and had
arrived at the hill about a mile from it, Perdy suddenly
put his horses into a furious gallop and Butler again
endeavoured to overtake him, both vehicles tearing
madly down the hill in a terrifying stampede. The road
was wide enough for the Chester mail to pass the Holyhead and all might yet have been well, if Butler, in
driving at a gallop past Perdy, had not seen fit to wave
his hat in triumph at the very moment when his leading
horses swerved in front of the other coach. The Holyhead
mail hit the bank at the side of the road and was immediately upset in a frightful tangle of broken harness,
rearing horses and screaming passengers. William Hart
broke his neck, Mr Archer was laid up for months and
another passenger, named Fenner, was 'taken up
almost lifeless'. Yet, considering the penalty for poaching
game was still transportation for seven years or for life,
the coachmen seemed to get off very lightly with a
sentence of one year's imprisonment.

In his summing-up of the case, the judge declared that
it was the duty of the coachman 'to protect even the
intoxicated, the blind, the aged and the helpless against
their own want of caution or imprudence', which was not
much help to poor William Hart or to Mr Archer nursing
his broken limbs. Even when he took his duties seriously,
the coachman's responsibility for the welfare of his
passengers was not an easy assignment. It depended on
what kind of company he had to carry on his vehicle, and
some of the intoxicated, brutish outsiders who travelled
on the stage-coaches were better left alone—or so it
seemed to Miss Weeton on her uneasy journey to
Liverpool in 1824.

Poor Miss Weeton—she seemed to attract awkward
situations by the force of her own unlucky and eccentric
personality. Her whole life was one continuous battle
with poverty and humiliation—first as a governess and

then as the ill-matched wife of a very shady character
from Wigan by the name of Aaron Stock, with whom she
had originally become acquainted on a coach journey
in 1813. Now, eleven years later, at the age of forty-nine,
separated from her husband and her child, she was at
last relatively free to please herself and, for several
weeks alone in London, had enjoyed the first holiday she
had ever known.

Her journey up to London on the outside of the coach,
which was all she could afford, had not been a very
happy one. It was extremely cold and wet and her
frequent application to the bottle of brandy a kind friend
had pressed on her, made her so drowsy that she was in
imminent danger of falling off the coach altogether. She
had no appetite for the potted shrimps or the cold
tongue the same kind friend had thoughtfully provided
her with and so was starving as well as being rather tipsy,
and when one of the horses fell twice in the shafts and
backed and twisted among the others as it was being
harnessed she was extremely frightened. Only her
precious wool-lined beaver gloves, and the other 'wrap-
pings' she had brought with her, gave her any comfort at
all. But she was all the more determined after this
experience to enjoy her journey back to Liverpool.

After much careful thought, finding the fares 'everywhere the same', she decided to take an outside place on a
coach going via Oxford, a town she had always wanted
to see. It left the Spread Eagle Office in Piccadilly at
half-past five in the morning and 'was very agreeable to
me', she wrote in her journal. 'The passengers throughout
this day were few and well behaved, the morning as
lovely as could be and the whole day's ride most delightful. Windsor Castle was a grand object, adorned as it was
in the early morning's sun. Oxford was a grander object
than I had expected; but previously to this Henley-
upon-Thames delighted me most; it appeared to be in

lovely romantic country. I was quite gratified with the
sight of Oxford, although upon a coach and never
descending. Yet I made good use of my eyes in the short
time we stopped . . . . '

Meanwhile, remembering the potted shrimps and the
brandy, she had provided herself with 'a basket sufficient
in buns and biscuits and a bottle of cold tea', which she
found a good deal safer, if not quite so efficacious as the
brandy in protecting her against the cold. At Leamington,
where the coach stopped for half an hour, she was glad
enough of being able to warm herself at the kitchen fire
and quite surprised to find the town such a beautifully
built and fashionable watering-place, while the sight of
the sun setting over Warwick Castle not only filled her
with gratitude for 'the beauties my Heavenly Friend has
this summer permitted me to witness', but made her feel
her soul was 'ready to burst the bands of the body and
fly upwards instantly to worship at His throne'.

It became still colder after the sun had gone down and
when the coach reached Birmingham it was quite dark,
so that all Miss Weeton could see was 'a vast number of
fires and lighted windows'. And here, alas, though she
kept her soul inside her body and covered her head and
face with a thick cotton handkerchief tied under her
bonnet, it was not the icy wind, or even the uncomforting
prospect of spending the night with a bottle of cold tea,
that turned her otherwise pleasant journey into a
nightmare. 'At the inn,' she wrote, 'we changed coaches
and took up 6 Irishmen of the lowest description, who
wholly destroyed the comfort of the remaining part of the
way by their selfish rudeness. One of them had usurped
my seat. I was quietly submitting to it, rather than
contend with him, but the guard took up my cause, and
a long scuffle ensued in which, I thought, between
them, they would overturn the coach. I then begged the
guard to say no more and rode the rest of the night on a

very dangerous outside seat, backwards. We were 4 upon it and it was too short by much for the number; but every seat was equally crowded. It was very necessary to keep my eyes open, for the least drowsiness, and I should have dropped headlong. The man on my left kept a constant motion with his head upon my shoulder, up and down, the night thro', being heavy to sleep, the brim of his hat endangering my eyes . . . . '

Another altercation between the guard and the vicious Irishman only made matters worse and, as if this was not misery enough, Miss Weeton was 'sadly bruised' from being jammed up against the iron rail which prevented the passengers from falling off the roof. 'About 6 in the morning,' she went on, 'one of the Irishmen in front left the coach; when I saw that, down I dropped and up into his seat like a cat and was much more comfortable, although I had one on my left as filthy as possible, and his head likewise jolting against me perpetually. It was intolerable! When I very quietly requested he would let his head nod on the other (the out-) side, I thought the man would have beaten me; the coachman then interfered, and they had a long quarrel, and at last a scuffle, as the driver was determined to hurl him off the coach unless he behaved better. . . . ' Poor Miss Weeton was so frightened, she burst into tears, but she tried 'to extract sweets from bitters' and to console herself when she discovered that her plight was no worse than that of the only other female passenger on the coach, who had passed an equally dreadful night with an Irish pig-driver on each side of her and another in front, snoring and resting their heads against her to prevent themselves falling.

How pleased both women must have been to arrive in Liverpool can only be imagined: Miss Weeton went straight to bed and slept until noon the following day. How brave such women were to travel alone in such company is often forgotten. It was all very well for the flighty or the pretty young women who could count on being well looked after by any gentleman riding on top of the coach, but for the Miss Weetons of the world—and she once confessed quite candidly that life was making her 'uglier than ever'—there was no redress, no security and no protection even in the golden age of coaching. The guards and the coachmen knew from experience with whom it was wise to argue or not; they could not be blamed if they sometimes decided that a weeping female on their hands was a lesser evil than fighting six drunken Irishmen and perhaps overturning the coach in the process.

13

ON THE
BRIGHTON
ROAD

THE BEST COMPANY was to be found on the Brighton
Road, for Brighton was to the beginning of the nineteenth century what Bath had been to the eighteenth,
the Mecca of the fashionable world and the gayest
resort in Europe.

Once an obscure little fishing village called Brighthelmstone, where the coarse black pigs from the down-
land farms came rooting round the muddy little stream
running beside the Steine and the sturdy boatmen
hauled their shoals of dazzling silver fish in from the
sea, it was not until 1732 that the first coach set out from
the George Inn, Southwark, on its way to the Old Ship.
The Sussex roads were some of the worst in the kingdom
and had scarcely improved since the days of Prince
George of Denmark's visit to Petworth. 'Never go to
Sussex,' Horace Walpole declared in 1749, 'if you love
good roads, conveniences, good inns, plenty of postilions
and horses. . . . Coaches grow there no more than balm
and spices'; and another traveller, Dr John Burton,

who fancied himself as a Greek scholar, asked in the manner of Aristotle: 'Why comes it that the oxen, the swine, the women and all other animals are so long-legged in Sussex?'—suggesting that it was on account of the extreme difficulty they had in pulling their feet out of the mud. None the less, by 1750, a certain James Batchelor was advertising 'for the convenience of country gentlemen etc', his London, Lewes and Bright-thelmstone stage-coach, which performed the journey (if God permitted) in two days, 'children in lap and outsiders paying half price'; and in the same year the little village by the sea was discovered by its first benefactor, Dr Richard Russell.

As a physician, Dr Russell was original, if nothing else, for his salt-water cure consisted in drinking sea-water as well as bathing in it, and the patients he persuaded to have faith in him apparently saw nothing fishy in this kind of treatment. Indeed, his cure very quickly became a fashionable and rather daring alternative to the taking of Dr James's powders. Persons suffering from melan-cholia, disorders of the stomach, vertigo and the fear of hydrophobia were all anxious to benefit from Russell's prescription. If it did not cure them, it should have killed them, since Fanny Burney, Mrs Thrale and her daughters were all ordered to plunge into the ice-cold sea before dawn one bleak November morning and were surely very lucky to survive such Spartan treatment. Hot baths, however, whether at Tunbridge Wells, Leamington Spa or Bath, were suddenly seen to be less efficacious for skin diseases, scrofula and other ailments than a dip in the cold ocean, and invalids of all sorts hastened to Brighthelmstone. They filled the Castle Inn and the Ship Inn to capacity and many of them over-flowed into the pebble cottages of the fishermen. These proved to be somewhat dank and smelly as lodgings and of doubtful profit to the health of the visitors, but the coach-proprietors saw an immediate gain in the numbers of people travelling down from London.

James Batchelor, whose coach still took two days with a night spent at Cuckfield, was furious with J. Tubb and S. Brawne, who started a very superior conveyance going from the Golden Cross, Charing Cross in one day and returning from the Castle at Brighthelmstone the next. Arguing that his family from father to son had put the first coach on the road and that 'many aged and infirm Persons, who did not chuse to rise early in the Morning, were very desirous to be two Days on the Road for their own Ease and Conveniency', Batchelor roundly accused Tubb of going much too fast and of attempting to steal his passengers away from him. A fierce battle of words continued between the two adversaries, until death robbed Batchelor of any victory he hoped to obtain, leaving Tubb master of the field for the next twenty years. And it was then, in September 1783, that a very gay and exciting visitor arrived in Brighthelmstone, who was to give the one-time fishing village an entirely new distinction.

If the twenty-year-old Prince of Wales, true to the Hanoverian tradition of quarrelling among the family, had not been on such bad terms with his father, King George III, Brighton might have remained the resort of the aged and the infirm and the black pigs—for it was mainly in order to annoy his father and to assert his own independence that the Prince first went there to stay with his disreputable uncle, the Duke of Cumberland. He found the freedom, the high jinks, the gambling and the heavy drinking in his uncle's household very much to his taste and, upon reaching his majority the next year, rented a house of his own on the west side of the Steine, destined to become, with all the alterations he made to it, a quasi-oriental pavilion of pleasure and his favourite residence in England.

Brighton liked the Prince as much as the Prince liked the sea air and the surroundings. His manners were charming and, at this time, he was tall and good-looking with well-shaped legs and an elegant air, his embroidered silk coat exquisitely cut and ablaze with French paste buttons. He could ride a horse with ease and dance a graceful measure, was seldom backward in any sporting or amorous adventure and enjoyed himself immensely. At the races or driving his own carriage—a new kind of phaeton called a randem—he cut a very fine figure, accompanied by his friend and tutor in driving, Sir John Lade, an eccentric young gentleman, who knew more about horses than anyone else in the kingdom.

Together the Prince and Sir John set the fashion in riding and driving, and the Steine became crowded with the smart equipages of the wealthy aristocracy, the *nouveaux riches* and the hangers-on of the fast set who found the Court of King George and Queen Charlotte intolerably stuffy. Curricles, tandems, tim-whiskies, buggies, barouches and britzskas drawn by superbly glossy, thoroughbred horses, soon outnumbered the fish-carts and the black pigs. Officers of the 10th Hussars from the near-by barracks hunted the ladies of easy virtue in light muslin gowns and beflowered bonnets, who idled round the circulating libraries and the taverns. Opulent stockbrokers from London, nabobs from the East Indies, gentlemen of fortune, French refugees and gamesters of all descriptions sauntered up and down, and the Prince rode or walked among them with a *bonhomie* none of his Hanoverian predecessors had ever shown. At the Royal Pavilion the dinners were enormous and Mrs Fitzherbert was a warm-hearted hostess to the Prince's raffish friends; the band played until the small hours of the morning and the wine reduced even the Duke of Norfolk, who could drink everyone else under the table, to a delightful, semi-glazed stupor wherein all the problems and anxieties of life were forgotten.

Meanwhile, Brighton expanded. New squares and crescents of bow-windowed, brightly stuccoed houses with elegant wrought-iron balconies were built to accommodate the ever increasing number of visitors, and soon after the Prince Regent succeeded his father as King George IV, the Chain Pier was opened with a flourish of trumpets and a firework display. The first of its kind in England, it quickly became the favourite promenade of the *ton* and of the more humble visitors, especially at high tide when the sensation of walking over the water was deliciously exciting. Tiny shops, built into the graceful towers, did a brisk trade in shells and toys of spun glass, in cut-out portraits known as silhouettes and souvenirs labelled 'A Present from Brighton', while at night, when the Pier was illuminated with thousands of little coloured lamps reflecting their brilliance in the water, it became a paradise of enchantment. Even the radical Cobbett, who disapproved of most things and objected very strongly to the dandies with 'stiffeners round their necks . . . their stays, their false shoulders, hips and haunches and their half-whiskers', had to admit that 'Brighton, closely bounded on one side by the sea and surrounded on other sides by lofty and verdant hills . . . is all beauty, whether as to the streets, the buildings, the carriages, the horses or the dresses of the people'.

The Castle Inn having been absorbed into the grounds of the Royal Pavilion and its licence given to the Royal York, most of the coaching business was now concentrated in Castle Square, where the booking-offices of the leading proprietors were situated. In the early years of the century the journey down from London was still a leisurely affair. Passengers entered a pair-horse coach at Blossoms Inn, Lawrence Lane, at seven o'clock in the

morning and had breakfast at the Cock in Sutton two
hours later. Next they stopped at the Tangier on
Banstead Downs, a rural inn famous for its elderberry
wine, made 'roking hot' by Miss Jeal, whose particular
pleasure was to serve the Prince with a glass when he
travelled that way. A light meal was eaten at Reigate,
where enough time was allowed for the travellers to
enjoy their food and to view, if they felt so inclined, the
near-by Baron's Cave where the barons were said to have
assembled on the night before they met King John at
Runnymede. Then there was a pause at Hand Cross,
where the landlord of the Red Lion, justifying his
reputation of being on very good terms with the smug-
glers at Brighton, stood at the door of his inn, bottle in
hand, ready to serve the coach with gin and gingerbread.
After this the serious business of dinner took place at the
Dun Cow at Staplefield Common. Pretty Miss Finch, the
landlady, specialized in hot rabbit-puddings and in the
summer the coaches pulled up under her cherry trees,
so that the passengers could help themselves to the
tantalizing black fruit hanging above their heads. Dinner,
what with the rabbit-puddings, the mulled claret and the
ale, took two hours before the coach went on to Cuckfield
and Clayton Hill, where the passengers, if their feet and
legs were still capable of steady motion, had to get out
and walk. A cup of tea at Patcham revived them
sufficiently for the rest of the journey and they reached
Brighton at seven o'clock in the evening, no doubt
famished for their supper and ready to devour the
several dishes of prawns and lobsters waiting for them.

But this leisurely mode of journeying was soon to
vanish when the macadamized roads made faster travel
possible and speed for its own sake became a glamorous
pursuit. The 'Comet', one of Chaplin's crack coaches,
cut the time of the journey to seven hours and then down
to six, and to travel by it was the snob's delight. Like

de Quincey, the young and the giddy preferred riding outside on a summer's day, the ladies with their straw bonnets tied on with coloured ribbons and their gauzy scarves flying in the wind, and the young gentlemen finding an easy excuse to slide a protective arm round them. The close proximity of three outsiders facing three more on the narrow benches at the rear of the coach added to the fun and the excitement, and more than one romance begun between Reigate and Cuckfield came to maturity beside the sea.

For some young gentlemen, however, the female passengers were less alluring than the horses, and their favourite seat was on the box beside the coachman, who could usually be persuaded to hand over 'the ribbons' for a suitable reward. C. J. Apperley, the sporting journalist who wrote under the name of 'Nimrod', confessed to having a mania for driving when he was still a schoolboy, and it was a mania he shared with the highest in the land. No young blood of the Regency considered his education complete until he had acquired the art of driving four-in-hand from one of the swell-dragsmen on the road, and all of them were ambitious to show off their skill on the most fashionable highway in the kingdom, hence the aristocratic amateurs who gave the Brighton Road a glittering panache not to be seen anywhere else.

Harry Stevenson, educated at Eton and Cambridge, turned professional when he put his famous coach, the 'Age', on the Brighton Road. For elegance and comfort it eclipsed all others and a crowd gathered in Castle Square every day to watch it setting off for London with Stevenson on the box behind his spanking team of a roan, a chestnut, a skewbald and a dun. Instead of brass-mounted harness, his was silver-plated, and besides entertaining his passengers on their journey with a flow of cultured and witty conversation, when the coach stopped on the road, his liveried servant waited on them, handing round a silver sandwich box and a glass of the finest sherry. Stevenson's 'passion for the bench exceeded all other worldly ambitions', but he drove himself too hard and died suddenly from an attack of brain fever when he was only thirty.

The 'Age' was acquired by another sporting gentleman, Sir St Vincent Cotton, an ex-officer of the 10th Hussars and a brilliant rider to hounds. Having already dissipated a large fortune at the races and in playing for high stakes, he took to driving the 'Age' for a living and made no secret of it, accepting tips from his passengers as any ordinary coachman would have done and earning some £300 a year out of his coach. Elderly ladies, who had known his mother, were somewhat shocked by this practice when they travelled on the 'Age' and those who were not aware of his aristocratic descent were even more shocked when he sat down to dinner with them and the landlord treated him with the utmost deference. Times had changed—not for the better according to the older generation; and as for the youngest of the swells, the Marquis of Worcester, heir to one of the oldest dukedoms in the land—for him there were no words left.

The Marquis, before he was of age, fell madly in love with Harriette Wilson, the queen of the demi-reps in London. From the moment when he first entered her box at the Royal Opera in the Haymarket and she allowed him to fondle her auburn curls, his passionate regard for her became the dominating feature of his whole existence and only the most strenuous efforts of his father, the Duke of Beaufort, prevented him from marrying her immediately. Instead he installed her in a house at Brighton, and wearing an exact copy of the 10th Hussars' uniform, she rode out on parade with him early in the morning to stop him lying abed and letting his regiment go to the devil.

Worcester was, indeed, captivated and enthralled. He

vowed he would rather give up his inheritance and drive a mail-coach than abandon his beloved Harriette, who was not, however, very keen on that idea; and once, while he was staying with his parents at Badminton, he begged her to meet him secretly at Oxford in the middle of the night. She disguised herself in 'a neat coloured gown, thick shoes, blue stockings, blue check apron, coloured neck-handkerchief, cloth cap and bright cherry-coloured ribbons' and pranced off in the stage-coach with a Mr and Mrs Hodson, a Mr Shuffle, a Frenchman in a light grey coat and a *risqué* Irishman. Unfortunately the cap and the ribbons did not prevent Worcester's uncle, Lord Somerset, from recognizing her when he happened to pass her on the road—and it was this same uncle who tore the weeping Marquis out of her arms and bundled him on to the Falmouth mail when he had been appointed to Wellington's staff in Spain. Harriette promised to wait a year for him in the country and herself travelled down to Exeter on the mail, wasting her talents for a while on the rural air of Charmouth and then travelling on to Falmouth with the intention of taking a ship bound for the Peninsular. But here she learnt, from a lieutenant of the 10th Hussars returning on leave, that Worcester was consoling himself with the frisky little wife of one of the Paymasters to the Forces, whereupon she journeyed back to London in haste and resumed the life of a 'Fashionable Impure'.

The Marquis came home from the wars in a wiser and more sober frame of mind, married the niece of Wellington, kept a white poodle and finally fulfilled his ambition of driving a coach when he put the 'Beaufort' on the Brighton Road in competition with the 'Age'. By this time more than forty coaches were running to and from Brighton every day, some of them taking only five and a half hours to accomplish the journey. All of them had the most high-sounding names designed to impress their

patrons with a sense of speed or to appeal to their snobbish instincts. Besides the 'Age', the 'Comet' and the
'Beaufort', there was the 'Royal Sussex', the 'Sovereign',
the 'Alert', the 'Royal Blue', the 'Regent', the 'Times',
the 'True Blue', the 'Dart' and the 'Royal George'.

Starting out from the inns in the city, most of the
smart coaches called at the West End booking-offices in
Piccadilly to pick up the passengers waiting there. Some
went down to the sea in search of health: poor Tom Hood,
the poet, when he was very ill, was lifted into the coach
at the White Horse Cellar, and the claret jelly his wife
had taken with them to sustain him on the journey
melted in the heat, oozing all over Mrs Hood's bag 'in a
regal purple stream' that got into her purse and made all
her money stick together. Some, like Hazlitt, honey-
mooning with his second wife in 1824, went to Brighton
to go aboard the steam-packet for Dieppe. Others, like
C. M. Westmacott, the scurrilous gossip-writer on the
London Spy, went down for the jaunt, to enjoy the ride
and a day by the sea. 'With what astonishment would
our ancestors survey the accelerated perfection to which
coaching is brought in the present day!' he wrote in
1825. 'The most sanguine could never have anticipated
the rapidity with which we are now whirled from one end
of the kingdom to the other; 52 miles in five hours and a
quarter, five changes of horses, and the same coachman
to whisk you back again to supper over the same ground
and within the limits of the same day. No *ruts* or *quarter-
ings* now—all level as a bowling green—half-bred blood
cattle—bright brass harness—and a well-bred gentlemanly fellow for a coachman, who amuses you with a
volume of anecdotes if you are fortunate enough to
secure the box seat, or touches his hat with the *congée*
of a courier as he pockets your tributary shilling at
parting.'

Westmacott, having arranged his excursion to

Brighton on the spur of the moment, sent his servant off to the Golden Cross to book him an outside place on the seven o'clock morning coach. 'Such a well frequented inn yard affords the greatest variety of character and entertainment,' he continued, going on to describe the back-chat among the passengers in the confusion of getting off. ' "Are you going by the Brighton, Mam?" "Yes, I be." "Can't *take* all that luggage." "Then you shan't *take* me." "Don't wish to be *taken* for a wagon-man." "What a cursed narrow hole this is for a decent-sized man to cram himself in at!" muttered an enormous bulky citizen, sticking half way in the coach door, and panting for breath from the violence of his exertions to drag his hindquarters after him. "Do we take *the whole* of you today, Sir?" said coachee, assisting to push him in. "Ish tere any room outside te coach?" bawled out a black-headed little Israelite. "Ve shall be all shmotered within, tish hot day; here are two peeples inshide, vat each might fill a coach by temselves." "All right—all right; take care of your heads, gem'men, going under the gateway; give the bearing rein of the near leader one twist more, and pole up the off wheeler a link or two. All right, Tom—stand away from the horses' heads, there—ehewt, fee'e't"—smack goes the whip and away goes the Brighton "Times" like a Congreve rocket, filled with all manner of combustibles.'

The box seat beside the coachman conferred a sense of superiority on the passenger who occupied it, which pleased Westmacott; it saved him from what he called 'the inquisitive and often impertinent conversation of the mixed group of inside passengers' and gave him a chance to admire the coachman's skill. Not that he ever tried to handle the ribbons himself—he was far too nervous of being caught; for, although it was so often done, it was strictly against the law for the coachman to allow an amateur to take the reins. Timid passengers, or those who wanted to make trouble, could report him to the coach-proprietors, who were in a very difficult position if the coach happened to meet with an accident. Juries invariably assessed the damages awarded at a much higher rate if an amateur was driving, and the coach masters found themselves liable for a very heavy fine; on the other hand they thought twice about dismissing a good coachman for a misdemeanour which was tacitly accepted as part of their perks and a privilege of the aristocracy.

Professional informers, who were very active on the Brighton Road in the twenties, made the position still more difficult. They were seedy individuals, without any visible means of support except for the money they scrounged by spying on their neighbours, and they deliberately caused the maximum amount of trouble by reporting the coachmen and the guards for overloading their vehicles or for some other infringement of the laws, which were so complicated anyway, no one except the informers really understood them. A man called Byers combined this objectional occupation with the running of a small shop on the outskirts of London and for a time did very well out of his snooping. He employed a number of still shabbier individuals to travel about as ordinary passengers or to sit in the upstairs windows of the inns, where, being concealed from view, they could watch the coaches passing by and report to him on their findings. Byers brought several actions into the courts against the coach proprietors, until, luckily for them, he went too far and, in spite of his ill-gotten gains, landed himself in prison.

For the timid passengers, alarmed by the frequent accidents on the Brighton Road, there were a number of patent safety coaches, one of them called the 'Life Preserver' and another the 'Sovereign', though whether they were really any less prone to accident than the usual type of vehicle is doubtful. The 'Sovereign' was built to a new and very curious design. No outside passengers were carried on the roof; instead they sat in an open kind of carriage set between the driving box and the body of the coach, and their luggage was stowed in a special compartment at the fore end. A large crowd of some two thousand people assembled in Castle Square to watch the 'Sovereign' start on its maiden trip from Brighton and the local press supported the belief that it combined the utmost safety with no loss of speed or comfort—an assertion eagerly accepted by the elderly and the travellers who suffered from their nerves.

To be involved in a coach accident was certainly a very frightening experience. All the eleven outside passengers on the 'Coburg' were injured at Cuckfield when the coachman failed to hold a fresh team of horses as they bolted away and crashed into a waggon, one of them, a Mr Blake, dying the next day; and even worse was the accident to the 'Quicksilver', which overturned as it was leaving Brighton, pitching the outsiders into the gardens of the houses in the Steine or upon the spikes of the railings, where they hung in grotesque and helpless attitudes until bystanders came to their rescue.

Accidents, none the less, considering the amount of traffic to and from the seaside resort, were no worse on the Brighton Road than anywhere else in the country. On one day in the summer of 1824, the coaches conveyed no fewer than four hundred and eighty people from London to the coast without any harm befalling any of them—and this was the year that John Constable first sent his wife and children to the seaside away from the suffocating heat and dust in London. On 5 June, before going down to join them, he walked out in the evening from his studio in Charlotte Street to book two outside places on the coach for himself and his young assistant, Johnnie Dunthorne, and on the 7th he was very busy doing up his painting-box and wondering what clothes he ought to take with him.

On the journey down, going by the new road through Redhill, a sudden thunder shower followed by a burst of sunshine over the hill and the windmill so excited him, he made a quick sketch of it the moment he got down from the coach, sitting with his paint-box on his knees and using the lid as an easel. Later he developed this sketch into the painting he called 'Summer Afternoon after a Shower'. And at Brighton he found the changeable weather with the storm clouds gathering over the horizon or the strong sunlight glittering on the bright sea, the fishermen lounging on the beach and the boats sailing in, highly stimulating, sometimes working on four or five outdoor oil-sketches in one day. He spent a week there with his beloved family, returning to London on 14 June on a coach that was full inside and out, with '4 females outside', one of them with a baby. 'The morning was very bad, but the day got up very fine, no dust, neither too warm or too cold', so that they all had a very pleasant ride, and since Constable had already been paid the highest compliment when it was said of him that he was 'always a gentleman at a coach dinner', the four females must have found his company delightful.

The next summer, after their eight-year-old son had been very ill, he again took his wife and family to Brighton, having reluctantly refused the Rev. John Fisher's kind invitation for them all to go and stay with him at Weymouth because the long journey into Dorset would have been too exhausting for the little boy. Brighton also had the advantage of now being within such easy reach of London that all through the autumn and the winter, while Mrs Constable was nursing the child back to health, her husband could travel back and forth to visit them without giving up his work in his studio at Charlotte Street. Sometimes he was rather annoyed at the amount of time wasted by the coach hanging about in Piccadilly before it started off, but that was a small price to pay for the pleasure of seeing his dear family, and at Christmas he went down on the coach with a large goose for their dinner and bundles of toys for the children. Young John was fond of harnessing his rocking-horse to an upturned chair and, with his little sister and her pussy-cat sitting behind on a second upturned chair, imagined he was driving a coach, while quite unaware that his father was sketching him at his absorbing game.

He recovered completely in the strong sea air, and in the following September, when Maria Constable was expecting another baby, his father took him back to Brighton to stay with their friend, Mr Phillips. 'We had a comfortable ride, and John was very good and quiet,' he wrote in a letter to his wife. 'I could very well have borne my great coat—and he complained of the cold 'till I tyed 2 silk handkerchiefs about his throat and a gentleman put his great coat over his lap. The ride and the effects were beautiful and it has done me a great deal of good. I wished much for you when I heard—and saw—and smelt the dear old sea.'

Absence from his wife was always painful to Constable and the joint care of their children his first consideration. When he took their little girl, Minna, as well as young John, down to Suffolk to stay with his relations in the autumn of 1827, he at once wrote off to tell her about the journey. 'We came inside the coach,' he said, 'with a gentleman and a lady who were very civil. Minna was sick but did not injure anything and was all alive at Colchester when I took her hair out of curl and washed her face.' Both children enjoyed the fun of travelling with their father enormously, and the next summer he took them down to Brighton again, hoping that the joy of seeing them would help his wife to get well. But by then Maria Constable was a very sick woman. Brighton could not cure her, or the air of Hampstead either, when Constable brought her home—and before the year was over, she was dead, leaving him with seven young children to bring up.

In spite of the constant demands they made upon his time and energy, Constable's tender affection for his children was so abundant, he never once found the task a burden. He was always devising treats for them, taking them on the Eton and Windsor coach to visit Fisher when he was staying there, or on picnics and other excursions, all the time observing with his practised eye, the sky and the fields and the landscape. Once on the coach coming through Dedham Vale, he remarked on the beauty of it to the two strangers travelling with him and was greatly surprised when one of them answered: 'Yes, Sir, this is Constable's country'—for at this time very few people in England really appreciated his painting and he was highly sensitive to the adverse criticism he suffered. 'I then told them who I was—lest he should spoil it,' he wrote in describing this incident to a friend, grateful for the unlooked-for compliment and anxious to acknowledge it without embarrassing his fellow traveller.

With its high, bright sky, Suffolk was the county he still loved more than any other and he constantly returned there, watching from the window or the roof of the coach the marvellous effects of the light over the familiar landscape. But after his wife's death, Constable never travelled on the Brighton Road again: the gay town by the sea held too many memories and he could not bear it without her.

14

FOREIGN TRAVELLERS IN BRITAIN

FOREIGNERS ARRIVING AT Brighton by the packet-boat, or at Dover, Falmouth and Harwich, were quite overwhelmed by the speed and efficiency of Britain's coaching service, which had no equal anywhere else in the world. The beautiful horses, smart vehicles and smooth roads astonished them. In France the diligence still crawled shakily from one town to the next. In Germany the uncovered coaches lurched along the treacherous roads at a speed of no more than six miles an hour and at each stage it took twenty minutes to change the horses, while the inns were dirty, fusty and derelict. By comparison England was a paradise for the continental tourist.

To Dr Niemeyer of Leipzig, the stage-coaches of 1819 were 'so great a novelty to all strangers unacquainted with the mechanical elegance and refinement to which they have arrived in England', that he was quite

enraptured by them and could not avoid giving vent to
the grateful feelings they excited in him by 'praises as
flattering as they were just'. All the way from Harwich
to London as the comfortable coach rolled along the
road, he was spell-bound by the beauty and the richness
of the countryside, the convenience and cleanliness of the
inns and the general air of prosperity he saw all around
him in contrast to the backwardness and poverty of the
European nations who had suffered for so long under the
tyranny of Napoleon; and when he reached London he
marvelled at its size, its grandeur and the constant
activity going on in the streets, especially at night, when
the gas lamps and the coloured flasks, shining in the
shop windows of the apothecaries, gave out a startling
array of brilliance such as he had never witnessed on any
of his travels anywhere. Almost everything he saw
excited his admiration—above all the schools and the
hospitals built by the various charitable foundations,
whose work he had come to study and to emulate—and
the longer he stayed the more enthusiastic he became,
ever remembering his tour in England as one of the
most rewarding experiences of his whole life.

Not all of Niemeyer's countrymen, however, were
quite so enthusiastic. As early as 1775, G. C. Lichtenberg, the satirist and philosopher, had compared travelling in England with travelling in his own country and
had come to the conclusion that the easy progress of the
English coaches constituted a grave danger to the virtue
of the passengers. In Germany the roads were still so
uneven and the vehicles so ricketty, passengers had to
hold on for their lives; they had no chance to look about
them or to become more intimate with each other, being
constantly on the watch for the ruts and pot-holes that
any minute might overturn them. In England, with the
smoothness of the ride, young women especially had
nothing to do but gaze out of the window or make eyes

at their fellow passengers, while the fact that the travellers sat facing each other in close proximity gave the flirtatious an irresistible opportunity for secret intimacies in the pressure of a feminine foot against its masculine opposite or the deft entwining of hands and legs. An Act of Parliament, Lichtenberg thought, whereby passengers on a public vehicle would only be permitted to sit back to back instead of face to face, would be the only thing to cure the young ladies of their coquettish ways and to protect the young gentlemen from their wiles. But the German philosopher was evidently very susceptible to English beauty, for he went so far as to advise any foreign traveller, who found the ladies too fascinating, to return at once to his own country. The speed of the English coaches likewise came in for his condemnation, because he believed it was the cause of so many successful elopements. Romantic couples in Germany, where the coaches moved at a snail's pace, had very little chance of not being overtaken by their parents, whereas in England a runaway couple, once they had got into a fast coach, were 'as safe from pursuit as if they were travelling on a magic carpet'.

The hectic rate of travelling in England distressed another German visitor for a different reason. J. H. Campe, a schoolmaster from Brunswick, landed at Yarmouth after a very unpleasant crossing of the North Sea and proceeding by coach to London, described his journey as 'a veritable torture', wherein every comfort was sacrificed for the sake of speed. 'We were obliged to cover 124 English miles from Yarmouth to London in fifteen hours without a single stop,' he wrote to a friend, 'except about half-way, at Ipswich, where we were suffered to refresh ourselves for half an hour. Even the most urgent demands of nature had to be suppressed or postponed in order that there might not be a minute's delay in changing horses, which happened about every ten miles. If a traveller wished to get down for a moment, he was faced with the danger that his luggage might be carried on to London without him. The coachman seemed to recognize no other duty than to arrive punctually. Whether his travellers, whose money had very wisely been collected beforehand, arrived with him was their concern, not his. The fresh horses were harnessed in a flash and away we dashed without any inquiry as to who was on board. . . .

'This indifference extends also to the passengers' luggage,' Campe continued. 'In order that not a second should be lost, everything—trunks, boxes, packages— were thrown into the well like balls. Whether they fell on their sides or corners, or damaged each other, or were smashed, was not even a matter for thought. A request that a little care might be taken to avoid injury was simply ignored. No one pays the least attention or even deigns to reply. Everyone is concerned with his own affairs and has no thought except to see that the coach departs at the exact moment and arrives to schedule. The result, so far as I was concerned, was that on arrival in London my trunk was in holes, while a sturdy box, made of oak and strengthened with iron, was stove in completely on one side down to its contents.'

Campe was terribly aggrieved by this misfortune and genuinely bewildered by the amount of traffic on the roads and in London, where he actually counted on one occasion, fifty-two hackney coaches in Piccadilly, besides what must have been one of the first omnibuses carrying twelve passengers inside and sixteen on the roof, without allowing for the numerous babies and young children perched on their mothers' knees. Perhaps he was unlucky in finding the coachman and the guard on the journey from Yarmouth so indifferent to the needs of the passengers, or perhaps his pedagogic temperament did not get the best out of people. Washington Irving, a far more genial character and an American whose ancestry was partly English and partly Scottish, took a totally opposite view of the typical English coachman and described him in glowing terms, with his 'broad, full face curiously mottled with red, as if the blood had been forced with hard feeding into every vessel of his skin' and his figure 'swelled into jolly dimensions by frequent potations of malt liquor, his bulk further increased by a multiplicity of coats, in which he is buried like a cauliflower'.

At Christmas-time, when Irving travelled down to Yorkshire, the coachman wore his hat on one side and had a large bunch of Christmas greens in his buttonhole. The coach was crowded inside and out with passengers on their way to visit relations and friends for the festive season, and it was loaded with hampers of game and baskets and boxes of delicacies. 'Hares hung dangling their long ears about the coachman's box', and at every village when the guard blew his horn and the horses came clattering to a halt, the people came running out with more bundles and boxes and baskets containing presents for their friends and relations down the road. Three young boys with rosy cheeks, returning home from school for the holidays, shared the inside of the coach with Irving, and he found their incessant chatter highly diverting. They were full of excitement at the thought of seeing their family again, the dog and the cat and especially their beloved pony, Bantam, and their pockets were stuffed with presents for their little sisters. The coachman had charge of them for the journey and, being a very good-natured fellow, did not in the least mind being pestered by the questions they asked, or stopping the coach for them to get down at the end of a lane, where an old servant was waiting for them with their beloved Bantam, 'a little rat of a pony with a rusty tail'. Moved by their youth and their high spirits, Washington

Irving leaned out of the window, hoping to see their
arrival on the steps of the country house in the distance
where he fancied he saw their mother waiting for them,
but the coach went on and a grove of trees hid this
touching sight from view.

Everybody in the villages seemed to him to be 'in
good looks and high spirits'. The grocers' and the
butchers' shops were thronged with customers and the
housewives stirring briskly about, decorating their
windows with bright sprigs of holly; and when he arrived
at the inn where he intended to put up for the night and
drove under the gateway, he 'entered and admired for
the hundredth time, that picture of convenience, neat-
ness and broad honest enjoyment, the kitchen of an
English inn'. Gleaming copper pots and pans, decorated
with Christmas greens, hung round the walls; hams,
tongues and huge flitches of bacon were suspended from
the ceiling, and a great welcoming fire burned brightly in
the grate. A fresh, bustling landlady and her trim house-
maids were scurrying about, filling tankards of ale and
laying the table with rounds of beef and other 'hearty
viands' for the hungry travellers who had just arrived,
and nothing in the world, Irving thought, could have
been nicer or more cosy than the warm-hearted reception they gave their guests.

He was not the only traveller from abroad to find the
English inns comfortable and good, in spite of Macaulay,
who thought the faster the coaches sped across the
country, the worse the inns had become. According to
him, the more the pace of travelling was accelerated the
less need there was for agreeable places of rest and
refreshment on the road, while greedy landlords were
given a gorgeous opportunity of charging exorbitant
prices for bad meals eaten in a hurry, with hardly time
to swallow a hot drink without scalding the tongue.
Passengers had no alternative but to pay and look

pleasant when the guard was blowing his horn outside. Yet the travellers at breakfast at the Bull at Redbourn on the Holyhead Road seem to be enjoying themselves in the picture James Pollard made of them. A lady and a gentleman with their hats still firmly tied on, are being served by one waiter, while another comes in with two dishes of kidneys and bacon. The stout gentleman, who has taken his hat off, is making the most of a game-pie, and the child in its mother's arms appears to have eaten so much, she is holding it sideways to dislodge its wind. Another gentleman is trying to persuade a young woman to eat a little more, a second preening himself at the mirror and a third being shaved. Two others are stretching and warming themselves by the fire, while the coachman waits hat in hand for the tips he expects to receive. No one appears to be in a hurry or in the least agitated by the guard blowing his horn outside the window. Even the dog has time to sit up and beg. But the Bull at Redbourn, which was a very busy centre at the junction of several long-distance coaching routes, had a high reputation for its excellent service.

Foreign visitors, on the whole, just did not agree with Macaulay's gloomy view of the coaching inns. Count Pecchio, an exile from Italy in 1827, wrote: 'At every inn on the road, breakfast, dinner, or supper is always ready, a fire is burning in every room and water always boiling for tea or coffee. Soft feather-beds, with a fire blazing up the chimney, invite to repose; and the tables are covered with newspapers for the amusement of the passengers.' In fact, 'English Inns would be real enchanted palaces,' the Count added ruefully, 'if the bill of mine host did not appear to dispel the illusion.'

Prince Pückler-Muskau also found them far more luxurious than anything he had ever seen on the Continent. The most pernickety of men, he was particularly impressed by the washing facilities. 'On your washing-

table,' he reported, 'you find—not one miserable water-
bottle, with a single earthen or silver jug and basin, and
a long strip of towel, such as you are given in all the
hotels and many private houses in France and Germany;
but positive tubs of handsome porcelain, in which you
may plunge half your body; cocks which instantly
supply you with streams of water at pleasure; half a
dozen wide towels; a multitude of fine glass bottles and
glasses, great and small; a large standing looking-glass,
foot baths etc., not to mention other anonymous
conveniences of the toilet, all of equal elegance.'

The Prince was no less enthusiastic about the servants:
the neatly dressed chambermaids, who dropped a
respectful curtsy to him when they came into his room,
and the valets and the waiters, who were always atten-
tive—at a price. Tipping was something he did not
altogether approve of—it was so expensive—though he
liked his comforts so much, it was usually worth it in
the end, and at the beginning of his stay in England in
1826, he still had high hopes of finding a rich bride who
would be willing to share his castle at Muskau with the
ex-wife he adored and had divorced in a desperate
attempt to emerge from his financial embarrassments.
His curious quest did not succeed, for, in spite of his
charms and much to his surprise, he found English
women very antagonistic to the idea of marrying a
divorcé and living *à trois* with his former spouse in a
remote part of Germany. None the less, the Prince
enjoyed himself immensely in London and at Brighton,
and by an odd twist of fate, retrieved his fortunes in
quite a different way when his letters from England were
published and became a *succès de scandale* everywhere
in the world.

Pückler-Muskau admired a great many things in
England, especially the parks and the gardens of the
country houses, the mature trees and the lush green

meadows that still gave the landscape a ravishing beauty; and indeed, the first impression the foreigner got, when he arrived at Dover and began his journey to London through Kent, was of one glorious garden of cherry trees, apples and pears, with the hops tracing their delicate pattern over the fields and the smoke from the red-tiled oast houses curling up into the sky. Amadée Pichot, a young Frenchman with a passion for English poetry, landed at Dover in 1825 and was enchanted by his journey to London. 'If you wish to form an idea of the vehicle which conveyed us from Dover to London, you must banish all thoughts of the heavy rolling machines which daily depart from the Rue Notre-Dame-des-Victoires,' he wrote home to his family in Paris. 'Picture to yourself a neat coach, drawn by four spirited horses, seemingly proud of their fleetness and the good harnesses with which they are provided, a well-fed coachman on the box and a guard behind. Such was the equipage which I found waiting for me at the door of the Shakespeare Hotel.'

Pichot gave up his inside seat to a young lady with blue eyes, who was returning home to her family in Kent after a visit to Paris, and her smile was an ample reward for his politeness. Riding outside anyway gave him more opportunity to enjoy the country and it was more exciting. 'Our Automedon smacked his whip and we soon found ourselves on a fine road as smooth as the gravel walk of a park, along which our wheels rolled so softly that they scarcely left a trace behind them!' he exclaimed, going on to describe how more than thirty similar coaches were proceeding in the same direction. 'We outstripped some and were ourselves outstripped by others . . . a spirit of rivalry animating both horses and drivers in a contest that is continually kept up.'

Coaches travelling in the other direction were also constantly passing by on this busy road through

Rochester and Canterbury, some bound for Dover only,
and some for the Continent—for the English, mistrusting
the French diligence, often took advantage of the direct
coach from London to Paris. It left the George and Blue
Boar in Holborn and provided 'expeditious and cheap
travelling to the Continent', proceeding by way of
Dover, where it was put on board the first available
vessel to Calais, and thence to Boulogne, Montreuil,
Abbeville, Amiens, Chantilly and Paris. As well as the
usual guard, it was under the direction of a courier called
M. Sombrat, and the London travellers enjoyed the
convenience of not having to bother about their luggage
until they arrived in Paris. Whether they liked the
French when they got there, is another matter. They
sniffed at the dirty inns and the bad roads and considered
French horses quite contemptible compared with their
own.

It was ten years after the Battle of Waterloo when
Pichot arrived in England. Emotions had cooled and the
English were no longer quite so rude to the French as
they had once been, though by Gallic standards they
could still be horribly uncommunicative. Pichot spoke
English very well and was the exception to most of his
compatriots in being able to find entertainment on that
blank, dead day of the week, the English Sunday, by
taking the coach to Richmond. He thought the crowds
of young girls, all dressed up in their best clothes, and
the apprentice lads with nosegays in their buttonholes,
presented a picture of gaiety and animation. The agile
way they hitched themselves on to the roof, the shrieks
of the girls and the laughter of the boys, the quick wit of
the coachman and the sight of the boats on the river
when they reached Kew, all added greatly to his pleasure;
but he could not get one word out of the John Bull
sitting next to him on the coach. Even when he asked:
'Is this Richmond?' the man signified that it was by a

mere nod of his head, and it says much for the tolerant
nature of Pichot that he was not offended by this surly
exhibition of British insularity, nor did he allow it to spoil
his delight in the view from the top of Richmond Hill.

Being a passionate admirer of Sir Walter Scott, he
was determined to seek out his hero in Edinburgh,
travelling north by way of York and choosing the outside of the coach again, although it poured with rain and
he got very wet. His friend grumbled, 'eulogizing the
cushions of the inside place', but Pichot was quite happy
when they reached the Black Swan and he was able to
stretch his wet feet out in front of a roaring coal fire;
and on the way to Newcastle he continued the journey
outside, still in the pouring rain, while his friend, prefer-
ring his 'travelling prison in the lower regions of the
coach', enjoyed the company of an attractive young lady
going north with her father. They all met at the inns
where the coach stopped, Pichot retaining his good
humour and enjoying his trip, even though the rain
could not be reckoned 'among the number of agreeables
the dicky of a stage assembled'. He was lucky enough to
find Scott in Edinburgh and to be invited to Abbotsford
for a visit, which crowned his journey with success.

The French had a great affinity with the Scots; they
all went north, either to visit the laird of Abbotsford or
to wander round the Trossachs and Loch Katrine with
a copy of *The Lady of the Lake* in their baggage. Edinburgh by this time was a very fine city indeed and the
intellectual capital of the north. The New Town was
finished; the innkeepers and the coach masters had set
themselves up in style at the Black Bull, the Star and the
Waterloo, and the old days of taking a coach from
Drysdale's whisky-shop were over. Travellers no longer
had to put up with dirty or bad accommodation; the
streets were clean and the smells had gone. But Edinburgh on a Sunday was a dead city. The shops were

closed, the houses shuttered and the people at their
prayers when Charles Nodier arrived there in 1821,
with three young friends, who had lost their hats on the
coach journey from London. To walk abroad in
Edinburgh on a Sunday without a hat was almost, like
whistling in the street, a criminal offence, and the four
young men, with only two days in which to see the sights,
were devastated, until Nodier conceived the ingenious
idea of each wearing his remaining hat and going out
one at a time while the others stayed indoors. By this
means they managed not to waste a whole day and to
see as much of the splendid city as they could before they
moved on to Glasgow the next evening.

Nodier was equally impressed with Glasgow. He
thought the streets and the squares on both sides of the
Clyde were magnificent and the view from the new
bridge superb. Then he set off alone on a tour of the
Highlands, 'among a people who do not even understand
English and which I only know enough of to obtain the
contrary of what I want by means of ridiculous circum-
locutions and extravagant gestures'. Quite undeterred
by this difficulty, he succeeded in climbing over Ben
Lomond to Loch Katrine with a guide, who traced their
route 'across the country as a bird flies, over hills horribly
wild and through wet and cold glens ploughed up by
frightful ravines'—and although his excitement for this
adventure never cooled, it was hardly surprising if once
or twice he found his greatest comfort lay in the Highland
whisky, which gave 'the most suspicious water an agreeable taste and a salubrious quality'.

Another lively young foreigner explored the Highlands
in the rain in 1829 and was almost drowned on Loch
Lomond, but survived to memorialize his experience in
the Hebrides Overture and the Scotch Symphony. Felix
Mendelssohn, on his first visit to Britain at the age of
twenty, enjoyed every moment of his tour in Scotland.

He stayed at the Saracen's Head in Glasgow and described his journey from there in a letter to his family: 'We flew away from Glasgow on top of the mail, past steaming meadows and smoking chimneys. . . . Sitting on top of the stage and madly careering along ravines, past lakes, uphill, downhill, wrapped in cloaks and umbrellas up, we could see nothing but railings, heaps of stones or ditches, and but rarely catch a glimpse of hills or lakes . . . in the evening a thick fog, the stage running madly in the darkness. Through the fog, we see lamps gleaming all about the horizon, the smoke of manufactories envelop us on all sides; gentlemen on horse-back ride past; one coach-horn blows in B flat, another in D, others follow in the distance—and here we are at Liverpool!'

Staying with friends for a while near Liverpool, he continued his journey to London with the music of the coach horn constantly in his ears and 'at the furious English speed', which after a time made him feel grumpy, so that he did not want to talk to any of his travelling companions and fell into 'a quiet, half-dreaming, half-thinking, half-gloomy mood'. Then a curious event stirred him. 'It appeared almost like a magic lantern of chance,' he wrote, 'when on the second evening of my journey, the mail stopped because it met the mail from London to Chester, and putting my head out of the window in the deep twilight, I saw peeping out of the other mail, François Cramer and his daughter'—a German pianist friend who lived in London. 'Exchange a few words with them, then drive asunder and part for years or longer—such is the world, moving onwards, meeting, coming near, going far away,' Mendelssohn commented—and such were the chances of travelling: a moment seized from the bed of time in the hurry and the hurly-burly, never to be forgotten.

Mendelssohn was one of the few travellers from

abroad who did not complain incessantly of the fogs in England. Frenchmen, Germans, Italians and Americans all seemed to find the damp and the mists intolerable and fog was certainly one of the worst hazards coach passengers had to face. If visibility was very bad when the mails left London in the evening, the Post Office sent outriders with torches ahead of the coach to guide the coachman out of the city; otherwise he had to rely on his own skill and the instinct of his horses to find the road. Around the smoky, industrial centres of the North and the Midlands, delays were inevitable, and on one occasion the Edinburgh mail rolled over into a quarry north of Darlington, the fog being so dense the coachman could not even see the rumps of the horses he was driving.

Frost, ice and snow sometimes stopped the mails altogether, in spite of the strict regulations of the Post Office. In Scotland in 1827 and again in 1836, the snow was so deep it rose above the heads of the outside passengers and buried those who were inside in a deathly white tomb. Travellers on the mails were abandoned by the guard, whose duty was to carry the mail-bags ahead by any means in his power, and nothing could be done for them, except to make a small chimney hole in the snow to give them a little air. Some of them did not survive, others, more bold, staggered and ploughed their way through the shoulder-high drifts towards whatever shelter they could find. Yet passengers still set out in the winter, the wise ones with coats and shawls and rugs, bottles of brandy, two pairs of stockings on their feet and a double layer of underwear, braving the cold and risking the chances of freezing to death.

And, worse than the snows in the winter, were the floods in the spring and the autumn. Shortly after Mendelssohn left Scotland, rivers burst their banks and bridges collapsed and more than one coach with all its passengers was lost in the turbulent water that suddenly swept the horses off their feet. Outside passengers were not so badly off if the horses managed to stay upright; inside passengers had to stand on the seats and bend double to avoid hitting the roof with their heads, and even if the coachman got them safely across, they then had to sit for the rest of the journey on damp cushions with their feet in a puddle of straw. No wonder one seasoned traveller exclaimed: 'Give me a collision, a broken axle and an overturn, a runaway team, a drunken coachman, snow-storms, howling tempests; but Heaven preserve us from floods!'

15

INTO THE
RAILWAY
AGE

THE *ne plus ultra* of coaching had been reached by the eighteen-thirties. Speed, efficiency and smartness could go no farther. Coachmen, guards, innkeepers and the hordes of lesser folk who groomed the horses, greased the coaches, swept the stables or simply stood around gazing in wonder at all the activity going on in the big yards, all shared in the glory and the prosperity of these days. Never had the roads been so busy, never had the English travelled so far or so fast.

Southey, the Poet Laureate and biographer of Lord Nelson, came up to London from Keswick in the winter of 1830 and on 27 December went down to Lymington to stay with Miss Bowles, the lady he was to make his second wife some years later. He spent a fortnight with her and then set off for the West Country, afterwards describing his very extensive and somewhat breathless trip in a letter to a friend. 'Monday, January 10th. I got into the Southampton and Weymouth stage, which left me at Dorchester,' he wrote. 'From thence the next

day by a villainous coach to Exeter and by chaise to
Crediton. There I remained 3 days with Lightfoot and
met some of my proof sheets (literally) as I alighted at
his door. . . . I left him before it was light on Friday,
14th. in a sort of covered cart for Exeter and got from
thence on the mail to Taunton. At Taunton I remained
8 and 40 hours with my good old Aunt, the last remaining
member of my father's generation. And on Monday
evening after an absence of 20 years I arrived in my
native city [Bristol] and took up my quarters with John
May at Clifton. . . . Friday, 21st, after dining with
Joseph Cottle, I got into the Birmingham mail and on
Saturday from Birmingham to Shrewsbury, where Mr
Warter was awaiting me. I went to his home at Cruck-
Meole, 4½ miles from Shrewsbury and past 24 hours very
pleasantly with him and his wife. Getting back to
Shrewsbury on Sunday night, I was in the coach for
Liverpool at ½ past 5 the next morning: suffered a piece
of stage-coach roguery at Chester which compelled me to
take part of a chaise with Mr Dawson of Manchester for
the waterside; crost to Liverpool, found no room in the
northern mail, but got an inside place to Lancaster from
whence I posted the two stages to Kendal and arrived
there at ½ past 2 o'clock and a frosty morning. The next
day I reached home between 12 and 1 and found all
well thank God, arriving safe and sound myself after
an absence of 3 months and a circuit of 1,000 miles—
never better in health and spirits, never with a fuller
head, never with more work upon my hands.'

What kind of stage-coach roguery Southey suffered
at Chester is now a mystery. Perhaps it was similar to
Thomas Carlyle's experience when he left his young wife
in Scotland and travelled by way of Liverpool to London
in the summer of the same year. He was booked by a
Liverpool coach agent on 'a certain imaginary Tallyho
and went by *seven* successive vehicles', which sent him

'circulating over the whole West of England', so that he
set his watch by the Shrewsbury clock, saw portions of
Wales and had 'the delightfullest drive', but nothing to
eat except a penny-loaf snatched from the landlady of an
inn in Shropshire until he reached London on the
following day at ten o'clock in the morning, where he was
horrified to find all the eggs that his dear Jeannie had
packed up for him had been smashed to pieces. 'Villainous as it was, I could not help laughing horse-laughs,
when after leaving Birmingham, I came to see into the
mystery,' he wrote. 'There are men in Liverpool who
will *book* you to go by any Coach you like, and to enter
London at any place and any hour you like; and *send*
you thither by any Coach or combination of Coaches *they*
like.' Thus he came into London tired and hungry and
missed his brother who was waiting for him at the wrong
inn, and it was only by luck that the broken eggs did
not spoil the manuscript copy of *Sartor Resartus* that he
had brought with him in the hope of finding a London
publisher who would take it.

Carlyle's journey by such a round-about route
covered far more mileage than was strictly necessary;
fortunately the amount of time wasted did not cause
him any inconvenience. But for Macready, the great
Shakespearean actor, time was of the utmost importance
when he set off on his provincial tours. In the autumn of
1834 he covered hundreds of miles in less than a fortnight: by coach from London to Bristol to act in *Sardanapalus* and on to Swansea for a performance of *Werner*;
then via Cardiff, Chepstow, Gloucester, Worcester and
Birmingham to Chesterfield, where he acted Hamlet one
night 'to the dullest, most insensitive and brutish
audience' he ever remembered, and Virginius the next.
Returning to London for one day, he went out to his
home at Elstree by Billing's coach to embrace his wife
and children, and immediately set off again by the fast

coach for Nottingham, where, in spite of feeling tired and suffering from toothache, he thought he played Hamlet very well. From there he hurried on to Liverpool for a performance of *Macbeth* and in one week before going on to Ireland, played Sardanapalus again, Virginius, Cardinal Wolsey, William Tell and Werner.

Highly strung, with a violent temper and, for an Irishman, very little sense of humour, he found long-distance travelling very exhausting and seldom had any use for his fellow passengers. They annoyed him and often provoked him to one of his uncontrollable fits of anger, which afterwards made him feel guilty and ashamed. He preferred dozing or reading, or even learning his parts, to talking to his companions, though he was highly impressed on the journey to Swansea by an agreeable gentleman who succeeded in writing quickly and easily in a book while the coach was moving, by holding his right hand with the pen in it firmly down on the page. One of the passengers on this trip recognized Macready and he was flattered on his arrival at Neath when a crowd of people surrounded the coach, running beside it to catch a glimpse of him before he got to the inn. But being a public figure sometimes put him in a more awkward position, as on one of his later journeys down to Bath when, like Constable, he found himself travelling with a stranger who did not know who he was. This gentleman, declaring that he was a friend of Charles Kean's, started talking about the theatre and glibly went on to tell a story he had heard about Macready not being able to act unless he was loudly applauded all the time, and then, the manager having gone round to stir up the audience, being received with such continuous applause that he protested he could not act with such a noise going on. Macready allowed the stranger to tell his malicious tale to the end, the smile on his lips pinched and frozen, but for once he succeeded in controlling his fury and, instead of lashing out at the gentleman, calmly gave him his card, and with great dignity apologized for revealing his identity too late to save them both from the ensuing embarrassment.

On Billing's coach, the two-horse stage between Elstree and London, Macready was so well-known to everyone, such a disconcerting encounter could never have occurred. The actor travelled continually back and forth and was, in effect, one of the first commuters in and out of the city. After a performance at Covent Garden or Drury Lane, he usually got home the same night when the stars were shining or the moon was up. If he could not get a seat on Billing's coach, there was another called the 'Crown Prince' which was equally convenient, and as it was only when he got back to his wife and children at Elstree that he enjoyed any real rest and refreshment from his agitating life in the theatre, he found the coaches a great blessing. In the mornings if he got up late and scrambled out of bed in a hurry, he knew he could rely on the coachman to hold the 'Crown Prince' back so that he would not be left behind or arrive in London too late for the afternoon rehearsal.

Macready and Dickens, who were friends for thirty years, did not meet until 1837; but in the same year as the actor made his journey round the provinces, Dickens as a young man in his early twenties was working as a reporter on the *Morning Chronicle*, a job which took him here, there and everywhere at short notice by the night mail, the fast day coach or any other conveyance he could lay his hands on. Though in later life he looked back on his coaching days with nostalgia, he was by no means always so enthusiastic at the time about the sudden journeys he had to undertake. First there was the tiresome chore of going to the booking-office to get a seat on the coach. 'You enter a mouldy-looking room, ornamented by large posting-bills,' he wrote in his *Sketches by Boz*, 'the greater part of the place enclosed behind a huge lumbering rough counter, and fitted up with recesses that look like the dens of the smaller animals in a travelling menagerie, without the bars. Some half-dozen people are "booking" brown-paper parcels, which one of the clerks flings into the aforesaid recesses with an air of recklessness which you, remembering the new carpet bag you bought in the morning, feel considerably annoyed at; porters, looking like so many Atlases, keep rushing in and out with large packages on their shoulders; and while you are waiting to make the necessary inquiries, you wonder what on earth the booking-office clerks can have been before they were booking-office clerks; one of them with his pen behind his ear and his hands behind him, is standing in front of the fire, like a full length portrait of Napoleon; the other with his hat half off his head, enters the passengers' names in the books with a coolness which is inexpressibly provoking; and the villain whistles—actually whistles—while a man asks him what the fare is outside all the way to Holyhead!—and in frosty weather, too! Your turn comes at last, and having paid the fare, you tremblingly inquire—"What time will it be necessary for me to be here in the morning?"—"Six o'clock," replies the whistler, carelessly pitching the sovereign you have just parted with, into a wooden bowl on the desk. "Rather before than arter," adds the man with the semi-roasted unmentionables, with just as much ease and complacency as if all the world got out of bed at five.'

The agony of getting up at five on a winter's morning by the light of a flaring, flat candle was acute; the misery of walking through the empty streets with the gas-lamps shining mournfully in the damp and a cold sleet drizzling down, even worse—and at the Golden Cross

14

there seemed to be no sign of the Birmingham 'High-flier'. 'You wander into the booking-office,' Dickens continued. 'There stands the identical book-keeper in the same position as if he had not moved since you saw him yesterday. As he informs you, that the coach is up in the yard, and will be brought round in about a quarter of an hour, you leave your bag and repair to "The Tap"— not with any idea of warming yourself, because you feel such a result to be utterly hopeless, but for the purpose of procuring some hot brandy and water, which you do,—when the kettle boils! an event which occurs exactly two minutes and a half before the time fixed for the starting of the coach.

'The first stroke of six peals from St. Martin's church steeple, just as you take the first sip of the boiling liquid. You find yourself at the booking-office in two seconds . . . The coach is out; the horses are in and the guard and two or three porters are stowing the luggage away and running up the steps of the booking-office and down the steps of the booking-office, with breathless rapidity. The place, which a few minutes ago, was so still and quiet, is now all bustle . . . The inside passengers are already in their dens, and the outsides, with the exception of yourself, are pacing up and down the pavement to keep warm; they consist of two young men with very long hair, to which the sleet has communicated the appearance of crystallized rats' tails; one thin young woman cold and peevish, one old gentleman ditto ditto, and something in a cloak and cap, intended to represent a military officer; every member of the party, with a large stiff shawl over his chin, looking exactly as if he were playing a set of Pan's pipes.'

Dickens in his *Sketches by Boz* was writing of fact, of his own immediate experience as a reporter travelling about the country—to Birmingham, Ipswich, Exeter and Chelmsford to cover the bye-elections, or down to

St Albans, when the blind and elderly Marchioness of Salisbury set herself and Hatfield House on fire. To get to St Albans, after receiving only three hours' notice and having previously been out of bed until three o'clock in the morning, he managed to procure a seat on the Leicester coach leaving at eight o'clock, and then suddenly realized that he would reach Hatfield more quickly if he got off at Barnet and made his way across country in a gig—not that the unhappy proceedings he was sent to report on were brought to a very speedy conclusion, for the inquest had to be postponed until the charred remains of the unfortunate Marchioness were discovered after a long search in the debris; by which time Dickens was off again to Kettering for the North Northamptonshire bye-election, where there was almost a riot and he thought the electors were the most ruthless set of 'bloody-minded villains' he had ever set eyes on. He made elaborate arrangements to send his copy back to London by the fastest possible means—on the mail-coach in charge of the guard with instructions for it to be delivered immediately at the offices of the *Morning Chronicle*, or by hiring post-chaises to carry the packet, if he thought he could outdistance his rivals on *The Times* and the *Herald* in their efforts to be first with the news.

In his letters, he often complained of the cold and the wet and of feeling ill and tired with so much travelling; yet all the time, with the prodigious strength of the creative artist, he was absorbing and storing away in his subconcious mind every detail of his experience on the road to fertilize the seed that blossomed into the characters of his imagination. Mr Pickwick at Bath, Tony Weller, the coachman *par excellence*, and his son Sam; Nicholas Nickleby, David Copperfield, Martin Chuzzlewit, Mrs Lupin, the landlady of the Blue Dragon, and a host of others lying dormant in his mind, were ready to

burst forth and to begin their immortal existence in the
pages and pages he wrote at speed to keep up with the
growing demand for his work. With his immense powers
of observation, his genius as a writer, his superabundant
vitality and his humour, he surpassed all other writers
in his vivid descriptions of coach travelling in all kinds
of weather and every kind of circumstance. There was
Mr Pickwick going to Ipswich, with Mr Magnus worrying
about his hat-box and his red bag; Nicholas Nickleby
leaving the Peacock at Islington, with a crowd of
spectators standing around in admiration, and Tom
Pinch, who had suffered the hypocrisy of Mr Pecksniff
for far too long, setting off from Salisbury for a new life
of freedom. When Tom took 'the swaggering, rakish,
dissipated London coach, up all night and lying by all
day and leading a devil of a life . . . he could not resist
the captivating sense of rapid motion through the
pleasant air. The four greys skimmed along, as if they
liked it quite as well as Tom did; the bugle was in as
high spirits as the greys; the coachman chimed in
sometimes with his voice; the wheels hummed cheerfully
in unison; the brass-work on the harness was an orchestra
of little bells; and thus, as they went clinking, jingling,
rattling smoothly on, the whole concern, from the
buckles of the leaders' coupling-reins to the handle of the
hind boot was one great instrument of music.'

Here then, in the twilight of a calm summer's evening
with the moon rising, and with a bottle of wine and a
cold roast fowl provided by the worthy Mrs Lupin, was
all the glamour and the glory of coaching summed up
in fiction, if not in fact. But time was short. Dickens,
when he wrote of Tom Pinch's ride, was already aware
that the great days of coaching were numbered. He had
no illusions about the overwhelming challenge of the
railways. In 1839 he was 'led insensibly into an anticipation of those days to come when mail coach guards shall

no longer be judges of horse-flesh—when a mail coach guard shall never even have seen a horse—when stations shall have superseded stables, and corn shall have given place to coke'. Sensitive to the transitional flux of the world around him, he was prophetic and wiser than most.

England was changing. The Reform Bill of 1832 had diminished the power of the aristocratic landowners by giving some measure of parliamentary representation to the manufacturers and the middle classes. Industrialism was spreading, increasing the wealth of the country and destroying many of its amenities. Birmingham, Manchester, Liverpool, Leeds and Glasgow lay under a perpetual cloud of smoke. The air, the sky and the buildings were stained to a drab colour, lit by the infernal light of the giant furnaces pumping energy into the deafening machines tended by the silent and pale-faced workers from the surrounding slums. Matthew Boulton and James Watt kept their secrets; they possessed what all the world desired to imitate—a new, dynamic power. Yet the average Englishman still believed that as a means of locomotion, fast horses could never be surpassed.

The first threat came, not from the engineering firm of Boulton and Watt in Birmingham, but from a talented Cornishman, Richard Trevithick, who invented and built a small steam-carriage, which he tried out at Camborne in 1802. He perched an ordinary coach body high up on two enormous back wheels and designed a single-cylinder engine to drive it. At the rear end was a large boiler with a very tall funnel and a little platform for the mechanic to ride on, and, in front, another platform above the very small front wheels, with a tiller to steer them by. After reaching a speed of nine miles an hour, Trevithick's steam-carriage exploded, but quite undaunted by this accident, he built another and better machine, which he claimed would travel faster

than any horse-drawn vehicle. He brought it up to
London to demonstrate its capacity in the new Regent's
Park, and this—or a later version—was perhaps the
steam-carriage Prince Pückler-Muskau rode on. He did
not think much of it. He found the smell of hot oil on
iron more unpleasant than it was in a steam-boat, and
the number of stops and starts due to mechanical
failure excessively irritating.

None the less other inventors besides Trevithick
persisted in experimenting with steam-driven carriages,
the most successful being Goldsworthy Gurney, another
Cornishman. He was ten years old when he saw Trevithick's machine at Camborne and so inspired by it, he
devoted years of research to achieving a better and more
beautiful steam-carriage of his own. By 1829 he was
running his improved patent steam-coach on the Bath
road at a speed of fifteen miles an hour. Eighteen
passengers were carried on it, six inside and twelve on the
top seats at the front and the rear; but on the first
journey they happened to arrive at Melksham on the
day of the annual fair, whereupon a mob of shouting and
booing rural folk surrounded them and presently started
to break up the beautiful steamer and to injure the
unfortunate people on it by flinging stones and farm
implements at them.

Gurney refused to be defeated by this misfortune. He
went on making his machines to sell at £1,000 each or to
hire out at 6d. a mile, and in 1831 a regular service was
started on the road between Cheltenham and Gloucester.
Three double journeys a day were made, covering some
three thousand, five hundred miles in all and conveying
two thousand and sixty-six passengers back and forth
for the sum of £202 4s. 6d. in fares. The boiler, Gurney
explained for the benefit of nervous passengers, was
perfectly safe, being 'constructed on philosophical
principals' and there was no nuisance from the flues at

the rear, since it was run on coke instead of coal; but a lot depended on which way the wind was blowing and the boiler did not always behave very philosophically. When one of the steamers operating round Glasgow blew up in 1831, seriously injuring two young boys, Tom Hood wrote:

> Instead of *journeys*, people now
>   May go upon a *Gurney*,
> With steam to do the horses' work
>   By power of attorney;
> Tho' with a load, it may explode
>   And you may all be undone;
> And find you're going up to Heaven,
>   Instead of up to London.

In London itself, Walter Hancock, who had been experimenting on the same lines as Gurney, ran a steam omnibus between Paddington and the City, which was so successful, he presently augmented his service with two other similar vehicles. Then he started a service down to Brighton, where Macready saw one of his machines careering up and down the sea-front, but was much too frightened to try this new form of conveyance out. Who would not have been afraid at the mere thought of riding on this dangerous-looking, horseless contraption? Yet it was not the apprehension of the public or any lack of curiosity among them that finally put an end to the steam-carriage; the Turnpike Trusts, in a panic at the loss of revenue they feared would occur if coaches were run off the road, raised the tolls for steam-carriages to such a prohibitive level, that they at once became so uneconomic to run, even Gurney and Hancock had to give up.

The Turnpike Trusts, and the people concerned with the coming and going of the coaches all over the kingdom, had less foresight than Charles Dickens. They simply ignored the far more serious threat to their enterprise coming from the smoky, fiery, snuffling locomotive invented by George Stephenson. Railroads they knew were already in use for dragging loads of coal from the pit-heads to the iron-foundries, but a steam locomotive as a means of passenger transport was another thing altogether and quite out of the question. Even the select committee at the House of Commons, called to consider a bill authorizing the Liverpool and Manchester railway, told the self-educated and tongue-tied engineer that his idea was utterly impracticable when he first put it to them, and it was only Stephenson's rugged persistence and the powerful backing he received from the rich industrialists in the district that finally persuaded them to give his new-fangled notion a trial.

Fanny Kemble, the twenty-one-year-old actress daughter of Charles Kemble, rode on the Liverpool and Manchester railway before it was open to the public as the guest of George Stephenson. She not only lost her heart to him—she became wildly excited when the mettlesome little steam-engine rushed ahead as if moved by magic, wafting them over bridges and through cuttings away into the open country. She stood up and took her bonnet off to let the wind sweep through her hair, closing her eyes the more to appreciate the delicious sensation of flying in mid-air, and she was not in the least frightened. Later, on 15 September 1830, she attended the official opening ceremony, when poor Mr Huskisson, a leading citizen of Liverpool, was run over by one of the engines and killed, and the Duke of Wellington got into a very bad temper about it. He, in fact, was quite unable to share Fanny's girlish excitement for the railroad: the mob waiting for him at Manchester was more sinister than the French army he had faced at Waterloo, and the moment he got there, he was obliged to withdraw the way he had come under a strong escort of police.

Such an inauspicious start might well have doomed the Liverpool and Manchester railway to failure, but instead, it was an immediate success, carrying more than thirty thousand passengers a month, ten thousand more than all the coaches running between the two towns could have carried even when filled to capacity. It was also a victory for the engineers and the industrialists, for the new enterprise that was soon to change the face of Britain out of all recognition and to destroy her coaching service at the very moment when it had reached its zenith.

16

JOURNEY'S END

THE RAILWAY AGE had begun. Yet the passengers on
the coaches, the guards and the coachmen, the proprietors and the innkeepers did not see what was coming.
They still believed in their own superiority—they could
not do otherwise. There were the highways of Telford
and MacAdam, stretching out like a well-behaved
octopus from Land's End to John o'Groats, with a
constant surge of traffic on them: the mails with their
bright lamps, hurrying at speed through the night and
the elegant stages covering the ground from London to
Shrewsbury, Holyhead or Exeter by the light of a
single day. Nothing surely could interrupt this regular
means of communication, which after nearly two
hundred years of trial and error, had come to perfection
in the accoutrements of the coach, the splendour of the
horses and the rapid conveyance of the passengers.

The German historian, Friedrich von Raumer, who
came to Britain in 1835, maintained that Englishmen
always argued from cause to effect; because they had
the finest roads and the best horses in the world, they
believed by natural consequence that their coaches were
also unsurpassed for comfort and convenience. But he

did not agree. While admitting that the well-bred horses and the smooth roads ensured an incredible rapidity of progress on any English journey, he thought the coaches in Prussia were a great deal more comfortable. 'To all theories *a priori* on the outside of the English stage coach, I oppose the bitter experience *a posteriori*,' he wrote with somewhat ponderous Teutonic humour, further asserting that the outside seats were so hard and painful, a travelling cushion was indispensable. Even when the coachman on one of his journeys kindly lent him a cushion, he was not much happier, for it was 'swelled up like a sponge with the rain of the proceeding night', and although he tried to keep very still, in sitting on it, he 'sank down into the primeval waters', from which his coat-tails and the bits of straw that began to stick to the seat of his trousers gave him no protection at all.

It was, however, the *a priori* reasoning of the English that to a great extent was responsible for their blindness when the time came for them to consider the threat of the railways to the long-established supremacy of coaching. The success of the Liverpool and Manchester line was in some ways a local triumph, but even when the line from Birmingham to London was under construction between 1833 and 1837, the coachmen on the Great North Road would point derisively to the work going on and make jokes about the insanity of the people who thought railways would drive *them* off the road. Most of their passengers were of the same mind. Even if railways were suitable for moving goods about, no one in their senses would, or ever could want to exchange the thrill of the stage-coach for the deadly, dangerous railroad with its tea-kettle engine, its stinking fumes and its gimcrack carriages on wheels.

Only one of the great coach proprietors—William Chaplin—realized the ominous significance of the crowds of navvies working on the embankment between Potter's

Bar and Hatfield. He was now at the height of his power.
Besides the Swan with Two Necks, he owned the Spread
Eagle and Cross Keys in Gracechurch Street, the White
Horse, Fetter Lane, several West End offices and large
stables outside London at Hounslow, Purley and
Whetstone. His business was flourishing and famous
throughout the kingdom, and he had made a fortune.
For him more than for anyone else the dilemma was
acute. Should he resist the new railway and continue in
competition with it, or reduce his coaching activities
and find some way of coming to terms with the iron
horse?

A more agonizing decision can seldom have faced
anyone. Chaplin employed thousands of people and all
his life had been spent among the coaching fraternity up
and down the roads of England. Coaching was in his
blood, from the time he had started as a small boy to
help in his father's stables on the Dover Road until now,
when he was fifty years old, he had to decide whether it
could continue or not. With a shrewd idea of the way
things were going, he decided he would have to co-op-
erate with the railways to survive, and when the line to
Birmingham was opened in 1838, he at once took his
famous coach, the 'Greyhound' off the road. Persuading
Benjamin Worthy Horne to join him, he made a contract
with the new railway company to act as a carrier of goods
and parcels between the intermediate stations; then he
put his money in the bank and retired to Switzerland.
Six weeks in a foreign country, away from the coaching
business, strengthened his resolve and, when he returned
to England, he made up his mind to invest his large
fortune in the new railway line from London to Southampton. For a time it was touch and go and he may well
have wondered whether his decision was a wise one, but
he was soon making more money than ever before and,
as chairman of the new line for the next twenty years,

maintained the reputation he had earned on the road as a master mind in the transport affairs of the nation.

Chaplin's great rival, Sherman of the Bull and Mouth, acted with far less wisdom. He believed in his capacity for twisting events to suit his own purpose and for two years kept his fast coaches on the Birmingham road, cutting the price of his fares in a desperate attempt to outdo the railway. Before long he had lost £7,000 and his smart yellow and black vehicles were running empty. The people who had sworn they would never travel on the railways began to think again and to wonder if their opposition did not make them look rather foolish, especially when the Post Office, after so obstinately resisting John Palmer's mail-coach idea fifty years before, decided to keep up with the times by supporting a bill in Parliament authorizing the conveyance of the mails by railway.

This was the beginning of the end. In the summer of 1838 there were still fifty-nine four-horse mails in England and Wales and sixteen in Scotland, and the annual parade on the Sovereign's birthday of the twenty-seven coaches, that left the General Post Office every night in the year, was as splendid as it had ever been. But four months later, one of many similar advertisements appearing in *The Times* showed the way things were going. It announced the sale by auction at Bagshot, Surrey, on the premises of the King's Arms, of 'Forty superior, good-sized, strengthy, short-legged, quick-actioned fresh horses and six sets of four-horse harness, which have been working the Exeter 'Telegraph', Southampton and Gosport Fast Coaches and one stage of the Devonport Mail . . . The above genuine Stock for unreserved sale, *entirely on Account of the Coaches being removed from the Road to the Railway.*'

One by one the mails starting from London fell away like autumn leaves and the great spectacle of their

departure from St Martin's-le-Grand and Piccadilly was
no more. One by one the fast day coaches, the proud
'Tally-Ho's', the 'Highflyers' and the rest, with fewer and
fewer passengers to support them, dwindled away or
acted in the humble capacity of feeders to the railways.
Travellers had to accept the dilemma of changing from
one mode of transport to another, whether they liked it or
not. To get to Scotland in 1836, Jane Welsh Carlyle went
by coach to Manchester, train to Liverpool and, because
the sea was too rough for the boats to sail, by another
coach to Dumfries. She hated travelling, suffered
acutely from neurasthenia and bad headaches, but quite
enjoyed her first trip on the railway.

'On Tuesday afternoon I reached Liverpool after a
flight (for it can be called nothing else) of thirty-four
miles within an hour and a quarter,' she wrote to allay
the anxiety of her husband, still working at home in
Chelsea. 'I was dreadfully frightened before the train
started; in the nervous weak state I was in, it seemed to
me certain that I should faint, and the impossibility of
getting the horrid thing stopt. But I felt no difference
between the motion of the steam carriage and that in
which I had come from London, it did not seem to be
going any faster.' In fact, she was quite disappointed
not to be able to return to London all the way by rail.
'I do not know how I shall return,' she wrote, 'by coach,
air or sea. If any cheap and safe conveyance offered,
I should certainly try the air this time, for the other
two ways I have proved to be equally detestable—and
killing.'

Poor Jane! There was no direct route by rail—yet;
and she eventually got into the mail-coach 'with as much
repugnance and trepidation as if it had been a Phalaris'
brazen bull, instead of a Christian vehicle, invented for
purposes of mercy—not of cruelty'. After breakfasting
at Lichfield on 'muddy coffee and scorched toast' at

five o'clock in the morning, she arrived at the next stop some nine hours later 'more fevered than hungry' and, with only ten minutes to spare, decided to spend the time in combing her hair and washing her face and hands with vinegar. But in the midst of 'this solacing operation' upstairs at the inn, she thought she heard the mail going off without her, with all her luggage and her purse in it, so she dashed down the stairs and out, without her bonnet, and her hair hanging down like a madwoman, only to find it was another coach going out and that she need not have got into such a frenzy. Travelling 'by air' as she called it, was infinitely preferable to the horrors of being left behind by the coach and the nervous exhaustion she suffered afterwards.

Southey also found the railway convenient in the combined coach, train and coach journey he made from London to Kendal in 1838. After describing the arrangements, whereby the Post Office clerks travelling on the train between Birmingham and Warrington sorted the letters on the way, he wrote: 'Nothing can be better than the whole management as far as we were concerned. The mail coach from the Swan with Two Necks carried us to the station at Birmingham where a better breakfast than I ever before saw provided for travellers was ready for us. The train was ready by the time we had eaten it in comfort, there was no confusion respecting luggage, and when we got to Warrington, after 20 minutes tarriance, two mail coaches started from the place to the North. So we performed the journey from the Post Office to my own door in 28 hours, 5 hours of that time being employed in posting from Kendal to Keswick, the whole cost of the journey £7. 10s. each. The best places on the train cost something less than an outside place on a stage coach for the same distance.'

Here was the chief advantage of the railways—as well as being faster, they made travelling cheaper and

attractive to a whole new class of men and women who
had never thought of going on a journey before. Not only
did the fares cost less on the railway; there were fewer
tips to be handed out and fewer meals to be paid for
en route; and as for the speed—nothing like it had ever
been known. 'Railroad travelling is a delightful improvement of human life,' wrote Sydney Smith in 1842. 'Man
is become a bird; he can fly longer and quicker than a
Solan goose. The mamma rushes sixty miles in two hours
to the aching finger of her conjugating and declining
grammar boy. The early Scotchman scratches himself in
the morning mists of the North and has his porridge in
Piccadilly before the setting sun . . . Everything is near,
everything is immediate—time, distance and delay are
abolished.'

But not everyone took to the new form of transport
with such enthusiasm. Some people were frightened.
'I was very glad to find from your note that you had
reached home safely having escaped all the dangers of the
rail-road with its fearful tunnels,' wrote one traveller from
Brighton. 'I think of returning to London by the good
old stage coach, slow though it be; it is better to lose
time than to run the risk of being crushed to pieces in
those dark tunnels, when you have not even the chance
of saving yourself by jumping out.' Other people found
travelling by rail monotonous and more exhausting than
the coach, while some of the gentry, like the Countess of
Zetland, compromised with the railways in a very strange
fashion: she had her own private carriage strapped on
to one of the wagons at Darlington and suffered a
terrifying experience when lumps of red-hot coal,
showering down from the engine, set fire to it, and her
maid, in a panic, after climbing out, fell on to the track,
while the Countess herself hung on desperately until the
train came to a halt at Rugby.

And whether the public enjoyed the railways or not

made no difference—they had to accept them as time went on and the countryside became a network of iron. Ruskin hated them for spoiling the scenery around Buxton. Wordsworth, when the Kendal and Windermere line was opened, wrote in anguish:

> Is there no nook of English ground secure
> From rash assault?—

and contemplated leaving Rydal in the summer because the numbers of tourists and excursionists—a new kind of traffic altogether—disturbed his peace. But Queen Victoria told her Uncle Leopold that she was charmed with her first journey from Slough to Paddington, and soon there would be no alternative. The super coaches, the mails and the 'Highflyers' were fading out. The Edinburgh mail was taken off the road between London, York and Newcastle in 1842 and ceased altogether when the North British Railway linking the Tyneside town with the Scottish capital was opened in 1847. The Glasgow mail suffered the same fate, the Devonport 'Quicksilver' had been withdrawn already as far as Plymouth but continued to run on to Falmouth, and the pair-horse mail to Dover, the last to leave London, ceased to run in 1844. Only the slow coaches, the short stages and those that served the remoter parts of the kingdom lived a little longer, getting shabbier and more old-fashioned, the coachmen cursing their ill-luck and the tired horses jogging along on their dying feet.

Nothing—nothing in the world could bring back the Shrewsbury 'Wonder' with its spanking team, the Manchester 'Defiance' or the Brighton 'Age' with its gleaming harness and its swell dragsman. They were gone—for ever. Men like Dickens and de Quincey might mourn the passing of the golden age, when the roads were alive and gay and the passengers huddled in shawls

15

against the cold night air arrived gladly at their destination—but they could only mourn, they could do nothing
about it. Everywhere whole towns and villages by-passed
by the railways and deprived of the traffic on the roads
began to decay. Inns were put up for sale, coaches stood
neglected in the yards, the stables were empty and the
coffee rooms, where travellers had been used to eating
enormous meals of beef and mutton, kidneys and bacon
and gooseberry-pie, were tenanted by mice and spiders.

By 1842, the Bull and Mouth, with only three of its
seventy-three daily coaches still running, was a dismal
sight and even worse, according to 'Nimrod', was the
plight of Hounslow. 'Not a coach, coach-horse, nor
carriage of any sort to be seen,' he declared, 'and half
of the head inn—the Lion—converted into a shop!
Where were the well-known sounds—perhaps to the
right and the left at the same moment—of "Four horse
job coming: bring 'em out boys", and the smart bow of
Harry, the ostler at the George, as he cried out "All
right" to the "boys", some of whom had been nearly half
a century on the road? Where the four or five nimble-
fingered horse-keepers at one coach, and perhaps one
more at the "opposition", priding themselves on the
fifty-seconds' change? Where the loads of sweet-smelling
hay and neatly trussed straw, that used to be brought
into the town for the two hundred coach horses formerly
stabled there? And above all things, where were the
happy faces and the well-doing appearances of the people
themselves?'

Where, indeed—? The innkeepers were ruined and
their servants left them for other jobs. The coachmen,
fit for no other kind of life, crept away into forgotten
corners of the country, glad of any company willing to
offer them a drink and to listen to their interminable
stories of the road. The guards were absorbed by the
railways; the travellers had melted away. And the roads

—the finest roads in the world—were so neglected, the grass and the weeds grew upon them until they began to resemble the tracks they had once been in the time before coaching began. The rattle of the wheels, the thunder of the horses, the voices of the passengers riding high on the roof and the sound of the guard blowing his horn for the turnpike gates to fly open—all were silent and gone. Queen Victoria was at the beginning of her long reign and England was moving into a new era. A few aristocratic and sporting gentlemen continued to drive four-in-hand for their own amusement, but, for everyone else, the proud and prosperous days of travelling by coach were over.

SELECT BIBLIOGRAPHY

AUSTEN, Jane. *Letters*. Ed. R. W. Chapman. 1932.
BALLARD, Joseph. *England in 1815, as seen by a Young Boston Merchant*. (Printed in Boston, 1913).
BLEW, W. C. A. *Brighton and its Coaches*. 1894.
BOSWELL, James. *Life of Samuel Johnson, 1791*. 2 vols. (Everyman Edition).
BOSWELL, James. *Journal of a Tour to the Hebrides with Samuel Johnson, 1786*. (Everyman Edition).
BOVILL, E. W. *The England of Nimrod and Surtees*. 1959.
BYNG, the Hon. John. *The Torrington Diaries*. 3 vols. Ed. C. B. Andrews. 1934.
CARLYLE, Jane Welsh. *New Letters and Memorials of*, annotated by Thomas Carlyle. 1903.
CARLYLE, Jane Welsh. *A New Selection of Her Letters*. Ed. Trudy Bliss. 1950.
CARLYLE, Thomas. *Letters to His Wife*. Ed. Trudy Bliss. 1953.
CARY, John. *Survey of the High Roads, 1790*.
CHAMBERLAYNE, Edward. *The Present State of Great Britain, 1684*.
COBBETT, William. *Rural Rides, 1830*. 2 vols. (Everyman Edition)
COLERIDGE, Samuel Taylor. *Letters*. 4 vols. Ed. Earl Leslie Griggs. 1959.
CONSTABLE, John. *Correspondence*. Ed. R. B. Beckett. 1964.
CRESSET, John. *A Printed Letter from John Cresset to A Postmaster in the Country, 1672*.
DEFOE, Daniel. *Tour Through England and Wales, 1724–1726*. 2 vols. (Everyman Edition).
DE QUINCEY, Thomas. *The English Mail Coach and Other Essays*. (Everyman Edition).
DE LAUNE, Thomas. *The Present State of London, 1681–1690*.
DICKENS, Charles. *Works*.
DICKENS, Charles. *Letters*. Ed. House & Storey. 1965.
DICTIONARY OF NATIONAL BIOGRAPHY: Gurney; Hancock; MacAdam; Taylor; Telford; Trevithick.
GARDINER, Leslie. *Stage Coach to John o'Groats*. 1961.
HARPER, C. G. *Stage Coach and Mail Days of Yore*. 2 vols. 1903.
HARPER, C. G. *The Brighton Road*. 1906.
HARPER, C. G. *The Great North Road*. 1922.
HARRIS, Stanley. *Old Coaching Days*. 1882.
HARRIS, Stanley. *The Coaching Age*. 1885.
HAZLITT, William. *Essays, 1825*. (Everyman Edition).

Hood, Tom. *Memorials of, collected by his daughter, Mrs F. Broderip.* 1860.

Hutchinson, Sara. *Letters.* Ed. Kathleen Coburn. 1954.

Irving, Washington. *Sketch Book, 1820.*

Johnson, Samuel. *The Adventurer, 1753.*

Keats, John. *Letters.* Ed. Buxton Forman. 1948.

Kemble, Fanny. *Records of a Girlhood.* 1878.

Kielmansegge, Count F. von. *Diary of a Journey in England, 1761–1762.*

Lennox, Lord William Pitt. *Coaching.* 1876.

Letts, Malcolm. *As the Foreigner Saw Us.* 1935.

Losh, James. *Diary and Correspondence, 1824–1833.* 2 vols. Ed. Edward Hughes. 1963.

Macready, William Charles. *Diaries.* Ed. W. Toynbee. 1912.

MacRitchie, William. *Diary of a Tour through Great Britain, 1795.*

McCausland, Hugh. *The English Carriage.* 1948.

Mendelssohn, Felix. *Letters.* Ed. G. Selden-Goth. 1946.

Moore, Tom. *Letters.* Ed. W. Dowden. 2 vols. 1964.

Moritz, Carl Philippe. *Travels in England in 1782.* Ed. P. E. Matheson. 1926.

Neville, Sylas. *Diary, 1767–1788.* Ed. Basil Cozens-Hardy. 1950.

Niemeyer, A. *Travels on the Continent and in England, 1823.*

'Nimrod' (C. J. Apperley). *The New Sporting Almanack, 1843.*

'Nimrod' (C. J. Apperley). *My Life and Times.* Ed. E. D. Cumming. 1927.

Parkes, Joan. *Travel in England in the Seventeenth Century.* 1925.

Paterson, Daniel. *British Itinerary, 1771.*

Pepys, Samuel. *Diary, 1660–1669.* 3 vols. (Wheatley Edition)

Pichot, Amadée. *Historical and Literary Tour of a Foreigner in England and Scotland, 1825.*

Pückler-Muskau, Prince Hermann. *A Regency Visitor.* Ed. E. M. Butler. 1957.

Raumer, Friedrich von. *England in 1835.* Translated S. Austin.

Robbins, Michael. *The Railway Age.* 1962.

Selway, N. C. *The Regency Road.* 1957.

Shelley, Percy Bysshe. *Letters.* Ed. F. L. Jones. 1964.

Simmons, Jack (Editor). *Journeys in England.* 1951.

Simond, Louis. *Journal of a Tour and Residence in Great Britain, 1810–1811.*

Sitwell, Edith. *Bath.* 1932.

SITWELL, Osbert, and M. BARTON. *Brighton.* 1935.
SMOLLETT, Tobias. *Roderick Random.* (Everyman Edition).
SORBIÈRE, Samuel de. *A Voyage in England, 1664.*
SOUTHEY, Robert. *Letters.* Ed. Kenneth Curry. 2 vols. 1965.
STEELE, Sir Richard. *The Spectator, 1711.*
STRONG, L. A. G. *The Rolling Road.* 1956.
THORESBY, Ralph. *Diary, 1677–1724.* 2 vols.
TREVELYAN, George Macaulay. *English Social History.* 1944.
TURBERVILLE, Prof. A. S. (Editor). *Johnson's England.* 1933.
VALE, Edmund. *The Mail-Coach Men of the Late Eighteenth Century.* 1960.
VERNEY. *Letters from the MSS at Claydon House.* Ed. Margaret Lady Verney. 1930.
VERNEY. *Memoirs of the Family.* 4 vols. 1892.
WARD, Ned. *The London Spy, 1709.*
WEETON, Ellen. *Journal of a Governess.* Ed. Edward Hall. 2 vols. 1939.
WESTMACOTT, C. M. *The English Spy, 1825.*
WHITE, R. J. *Life in Regency England.* 1963.
WILSON, Harriette. *Memoirs,* 1825.
WOODFORDE, James. *Diary of a Country Parson.* Ed. John Beresford. 5 vols. 1929.
WORDSWORTH, Mary. *Letters.* Ed. Mary Barton. 1958.
YOUNG, Arthur. *Farmer's Letters to the People of England, 1767.*

INDEX